SENDING POSITIVE VIBES

SENDING POSITIVE VIBES

FR BRYAN SHORTALL

columba
BOOKS

First published in 2019 by

columbaBOOKS

23 Merrion Square

Dublin 2, Ireland

www.columbabooks.com

ISBN: 978-1-78218-367-9

Set in Freight Text Pro 11/14 and Stefont
Cover and book design by Alba Esteban | Columba Books
Front cover photograph by Alexis Sierra
Printed by Jellyfish Solutions

Contents

Acknowledgements

I am forever grateful to Br Sean Kelly OFM Cap., Provincial Minister, and my Capuchin brothers.

To the parishioners of St Francis of Assisi, Priorswood, and St Michan's, Halston Street, for their support.

I deeply appreciate the support and encouragement of Archbishop Diarmuid Martin in both this book and the first one.

I wish to thank my own family for their support and advice in putting together the text.

To my dad, Enda, and to my mother, Bernadette. All her life, my mother has been an avid reader. She loves books and she knows books. Mam, thanks for your honesty and encouragement. You need to finish that book you've been writing!

Thanks to Erica Doyle Higgins for offering to read the text and for asking me how it's going.

Like the first book, thanks to Paddy Pender for the huge support in reading the text and offering advice and guidance from the start.

I am honoured that my brother, Kevin Shortall wrote a piece as an epilogue for this book. It is a powerful reflection written from my own family's perspective. Along with my other siblings, Gráinne, David, Aoife, Lorna and Clodagh, he was with me every step of the way. Kev, you need to write that book too bro!

Thanks to Garry O'Sullivan and the Columba Books team for the support and for believing in me.

I am deeply grateful to Br Kevin Crowley OFM Cap., for submitting the thought-provoking foreword for this book and for his encouragement along the way.

I dedicate this book to my Capuchin brothers and to Sam, Louise, Jane, Orlagh and Ross.

Fr Bryan Shortall OFM Cap.
Dublin, autumn 2019

Foreword

We started the Capuchin Day Centre in 1969 for the purpose of giving the homeless men at the time somewhere warm to go when they left the hostels in the mornings. Initially it started small and over the years the needs changed and grew. Today, in its 50th year, the Centre is expanding to meet the ever-increasing needs of the homeless and especially homeless families. It's a scandal that the problem seems to be getting worse rather than better and the stark statistics don't just speak for themselves – they cry out from the rooftops and across all media platforms. But there is hope; there's always hope.

Br. Bryan Shortall, now Parish Priest in St Francis of Assisi Parish, Priorswood, was based here in Church Street and Halston Street for the last nine years. We worked together in the Capuchin Community in Church Street. Like all followers of Saint Francis of Assisi, he tries to focus on the call of Jesus Christ to 'Repair my Church'. Francis of Assisi initially thought that call meant repairing the church building, block by block, and stone by stone, with bricks and mortar. Later, it emerged that it was about helping people made in the image and likeness of God – especially the poorest and most vulnerable.

The reflections here in this book, and in Bryan's first book, *Tired of all the Bad News*, try to convey the positive message of the Gospel as just that – good news in the world of the 21st century. He tells this through homilies, reflections, and stories he's heard along the way. In this book too, he tells something of his own story growing up in Dublin city.

9

The wonderful occasion of the visit of Pope Francis to the Capuchin Day Centre, just a year ago, where Bryan was present with other friars, reminded us of the pope's care and love for the poor and how this is reflected in his words and actions. Here in the Day Centre on the 25 August 2018, the Holy Father applauded the spirit of the ministry of the Centre when he said: 'You are especially attuned with the people of God, and indeed, with the poor. You have the grace of contemplating the wounds of Jesus in those in need, those who suffer, and those who are unfortunate or destitute, or full of vices or defects. For you, it is the flesh of Christ ... Another thing you said touched my heart. That you don't ask any questions. You accept life as it comes, you give comfort, and if need be you forgive.' Pope Francis has used the image of church being a 'field hospital', treating and binding wounds and welcoming all people. This is what we endeavour to do going forward in the Capuchin Day Centre as we celebrate our Golden Jubilee this year 2019.

I wish Bryan well as he continues in his own Capuchin life and ministry to repair the church of Jesus Christ after the example of Francis of Assisi and reinforced in the ministry of Pope Francis. We have tried to do this over the years in the Centre and, in truth, while there have been tough times and times of difficulty, it has always been a privilege and a joy to serve the people of God along with our committed staff and volunteers.

I am confident that this book will be another way for people to see the love and care of Jesus for all and especially the most vulnerable.

Br Kevin Crowley OFM Cap.
Founder/CEO/Co-Director
Capuchin Day Centre for Homeless, Dublin 7

Introduction

The first book was *Tired of all the Bad News* which came out at the end of 2016. Columba Books had asked me to submit a foreword to a book they published on Padre Pio. They were happy with the piece I'd written, and they said they would like to return the favour some time. I said; 'Maybe you can.' I admit this as a friar but in truth, it was an exercise in vanity! I had a bunch of essays, reflections and homilies, some blogged, since 2012. They said 'Send them in.' After a conversation with the Provincial Minister, I emailed text to Columba and the thing took shape. Joe Duffy kindly wrote the foreword and later launched it in March 2017.

When I saw the cover first, and then got my hands on two copies of it, it frightened the life out of me. For a few weeks after, I found myself reading it and noticing what I thought were mistakes and I imagined having to explain myself to people. Paddy Pender told me to stop reading it! I believe it was well received overall and so much so that it went to a second printing.

And then we come to this one. Tongue in cheek, I was giving this text the working title of 'Thinks he's better than he is'. In school, one of my teachers in fifth and sixth year said to me; 'You think you're better than you are.' That was possibly true, except in maths. He put it into his comments on one of my Christmas reports

Both Columba and my family were eager that I tell more of my story, which is what I intended to do. I guess it's a bit of the story of my life and how I became a Capuchin Franciscan and some more reflections and homilies I've given along the way. It's no secret that Pope St John Paul II has had a big influence on my life and vocation. From the strong youthful man I saw fly into Dublin on the Aer Lingus Jumbo Jet in 1979 when I was almost 10 years old, to the old and weak man I saw in Rome at the canonisation of St Padre Pio in 2002. This has now been book-ended in 2018 in the Capuchin Day Centre when, with Br Kevin and the other friars, I met Pope Francis personally. It was without doubt one of the most memorable days of my life and I will never forget it.

From the beginning of his pontificate, Pope Francis would ask everyone: 'Don't forget to pray for me.' On one occasion, I recall he added something like; ' … And if you don't pray, please send me your positive thoughts.' It seems to me in order to keep the good news going, we need to send out these positive vibes and thoughts as much as possible.

Little did we Know

A PSALM OF THE SIGHTS AND SOUNDS OF MY CHILDHOOD

Visiting an elderly parishioner - a lifelong smoker. The smell of cigarettes all around the room. It was strangely comforting. It was like a time-machine. I was taken back to my childhood.

Government warning: 'Smoking can damage your health' it said on the side of the cigarette pack. We'd stop at the late shop on the way home. 'Ten number 6, please.'

The sights, sounds and smells of Dublin in the late 1970s. It was noisy in the city except on Sundays, most shops were closed on Sundays. More noise but less busy.

Petrol. The Honda 50 motorbike could be heard before it was seen, and the smell of its exhaust lingered long after it disappeared around the corner and out of sight. The black and white Atlantean CIE Buses belching out diesel. Getting on the bus, the conductor, with his leather satchel full of coins and his ticket machine, would say, 'Seats on the top'. And smoking was allowed upstairs. Drawing finger pictures on the window in the cold and wet condensation and wiping it to see outside as we drove along on a rainy day. The sporadic 'ding' of the bell as people signalled to the driver they wanted to get off. 'Do not cross the white line until the bus stops.' The hissing of the doors as they opened.

The coal fire at home. My mother putting newspaper against it to try and light the fire. Smoke going up the chimney. And if the door opened the smoke would fill the sitting room. Pungent but homely. Doing the dishes in the sink. Look up. The noise of the Aer Lingus BAC 1-11 overhead as its tail almost rips through the sky. Outside on a frosty evening the smog would hang like a blanket over the houses in the city and over the 'chimbley' pots and television aerials.

Nana's stew: unique and delicious. And her mashed potato, milky and buttery. Pork chops and baked beans. Grandpop sitting by the fire preparing his pipe. Condor plug. He cut the tobacco with his little knife, the flake dropping into the V he made with a page of the *Evening Press*. Then when the pipe was filled and lit, he would do the crossword, reaching into his sideboard for the *Collins Gem Dictionary*. The pipe smoke rising like incense mixing with the smoke of Mr Dowling's coal. The pig man calls, and Nana brings out a pale pink bucket of slop. Yesterday's stew, potato peels, beans, and he spills it into one of his big steel bins. 'Thanks missus.'

The Ferguson television goes on – or was it Bush? RTÉ News. This was the second news bulletin I would have seen. Around in Auntie Chrissy's she would have been watching *Crossroads*. Then the News at 5.45 with Alastair Burnett. Back to Nana's and the Angelus would be ringing and then Maurice O'Doherty would read the News. Or Don Cockburn. 'The Taoiseach Mr Cosgrave said today ... '

Going to the shops. The shopkeeper writes how much with a pencil on a brown paper bag. No cash register. Peggy's Leg. Big Time bar. Dairy Milk. A tin of Coke. Cool pops. HB Loop the Loop for 6p. Iced Caramels. Clove rock. Sherbet dip and fizz. Snap gum. TK Red Lemonade and Ciderette. We used to return the empty glass bottles for three pence.

Going to the Chemist. Unique Smell. Almost indescribable in words but you know what I mean; wood and ointment. Barley sugar. Radiomulsion.

The hardware shop where Frank Russell sold Crown paints, or Valspar, or Berger. My dad had to open the tin with a flat-head screwdriver and stir it for ages. Ultra-Brilliant White it said on the tin. He had a lamp for sale. 'See that, Enda – it would look better in your sitting room than in my shop.'

I loved the smell of the back of the Brennan's Bread van. And Jacob's biscuit factory. We just knew when they were making Mikado. Jam in the air.

Running down to the gap at the end of our road. The JCB and the dumper were moving up by the pylon. The smell of brown topsoil and the yellow of the rapeseed flower giving way to house foundations as Kilnamanagh estate expands and takes shape. Sliding down the hill in the snow on a Net Nitrate bag. The girls played 'beds' with a shoe polish 'piggy' and swung on lampposts. The lads played 'three-and-in' and we all played Relieve-io and Spin-the-bottle. 'Eeenie, meanie, miny, mo ... '.

The milkman coming around the neighbourhood in the dark of the early morning. The clink of glass bottles dancing on the doorsteps. He takes away the empties. Battery-powered milk float.

The smell of a wet day. Newspapers soaking up the water on the shop floor. And sawdust; there was sawdust all over the butcher's shop floor, and the smell of breadcrumbs. The days of the separate pork butcher and the beef butcher shops were coming to an end. 'Give us six nice slices of ham, Mister.' And Frawley's on Thomas Street. The Frawley's club dressed us all for Christmas. Never could people have imagined the pope driving down past John's Lane in his popemobile – but he did.

The bee-baw of the white ambulance. The dark blue Garda cars and the 'Black Maria'. My Dad's Mini Traveller JNI 69. Give her choke on a cold day. A mystery tour to the Old Boley Wood in the mountains in the summer. Flo Gas and boil the teapot. Tayto crisps. Ham sandwiches, salad sandwiches. Cadet cola.

Tomato sandwiches with pepper in Granny Greta's. Starving after our swim in Vincent's pool. *The Riordans* would have been on;

Benjy and Minnie. The light of the Geyser flickering at the far end of the kitchen. Turn on the taps in the bathroom, the whisper of the water flowing down the drain. We found a gas mask as we explored the attic. And old shoes.

The smell of school and the corridors and the blackboard and dusty chalk. Pale blue desks in St Kevin's. Old wooden desks with ink wells in James's Street. Names scratched with set squares into the area underneath as well as chewing gum and stale bread stuck under the desks. Bubble-gum. Super Bazooka and Bubblicious. New schoolbooks and second-hand ones too, covered in wallpaper or brown wrapper. Capital Exercise Book 88 pages. 'Guaranteed Irish'. Milk bottles being delivered outside the door. Freezing corned beef sandwiches on Monday, buns on Wednesday, and jam on Friday. I couldn't drink milk. Snorkel jackets and Duffel coats. Dozens of ETs walking home after school.

What was on the Radio? Larry Gogan, Gaybo, Abba, The Nolan sisters, The Bee Gees, The King is Dead. Pirate Stations. On the telly? *Who shot J.R.?*, *The Late Late*, *Going Strong*, *Quicksilver*, *Wanderly Wagon*, *Mart and Market*, *Charlie's Angels*, *Quincy*, *The Professionals*, *The Six Million Dollar Man*, *The Multi-Coloured Swap Shop*, and then *Closedown*. In the Cinema? *Jaws* in the Adelphi and *Saturday Night Fever* in the Savoy.

Little did we know that the city would become busy on Sundays.

Little did we know that Jervis Street Hospital would become a shopping centre.

Little did we know that there would be a soccer game played in Croke Park.

Little did we know smoking would become anti-social.

Little did we know the Quays would become one-way systems.

Little did we know that Dublin Docklands would be the place to live and work.

Little did we know that in the future we would laugh at the thoughts of the telephone on the hall table at the bottom of the stairs.

Little did we know one day we would access the world on a portable device the size of a calculator and immediately be able to tell everyone on our timeline about our day.

Little did we know in the future we would buy bottled water.

Little did we know about the revolution that was soon to happen in Irish air travel.

Little did we know about Google.

Little did we know ...

Light out of Darkness

I wrote this homily a few years ago when Pope Francis travelled to World Youth Day in Krakow, Poland. World Youth Day is an opportunity for the pope to meet with young people from all across the globe. WYD, as many refer to it, takes place every few years and generally different continents get to host it. Huge numbers of a million strong turn up, especially for the Evening Prayer gathering with the pope and for the Mass on the Sunday morning. While prayer is important, it is also important for young people to be together and to connect in song, dance, story, and over food and hospitality. Like music festivals, the huge stage rigs are put in place and the sound and vision systems are erected so that everyone will see and hear the pope. At the end of many World Youth Days, there have been fireworks displays and a carnival atmosphere.

Holding the week-long youth event in Poland this time was to focus the attention on Europe. The aim was also to celebrate the Polish pope who 'invented' World Youth Day, John Paul II. I write about my experience of having attended a WYD in 2005 in Cologne, Germany, elsewhere in this book. What an experience! It was the summer that we said goodbye to John Paul and hello to Benedict. I was blown away by the sheer numbers of young people and the noise of the Masses. To listen to some who would lament that the churches are empty, and the young people go nowhere near the church, going to WYD would knock that right out of the park – it's mega.

So here it is:

Over this weekend at our Masses, we will spiritually join over a million young people from all over the world gathered with Pope Francis in Krakow for the World Youth Day celebrations. Since Pope St John Paul II inaugurated the concept of special meetings between the pope and young people in the 1980s, World Youth Day has visited all five continents and Popes John Paul, Benedict, and now Francis have met with millions of young people for prayer, catechesis and reconciliation.

This WYD is being celebrated in the midst of the Jubilee Year of Mercy, called by Pope Francis last year. It is taking place in Krakow near the home of Divine Mercy and in the heart of Pope John Paul's home city. There have been very moving scenes of Pope Francis walking through the gates of Auschwitz, where perhaps the worst kinds of evil were perpetrated upon men, women and children during the Second World War. Francis is the third pope to come to Auschwitz and to simply pray in profound solidarity with survivors and their families today. Pope John Paul II had personal experiences of Auschwitz during the war as friends of his were taken there and murdered. Later as archbishop and then as pope (in 1979) he visited Auschwitz and he wrote these powerful words:

> I have come, and I kneel on this Golgotha of the modern world, on these tombs, largely nameless like the great tomb of the Unknown Soldier. I kneel before all the inscriptions that come one after another bearing the memory of the victims of Birkenau in languages: Polish, English, Bulgarian, Romany, Czech, Danish, French, Greek, Hebrew, Yiddish, Spanish, Flemish, Serbo-Croat, German, Norwegian, Russian, Romanian, Hungarian and Italian.

In particular I pause with you, dear participants in this encounter, before the inscription in Hebrew. This inscription awakens the memory of the People whose sons and daughters were intended for total extermination. This People draws its origin from Abraham, our father in faith (cf. Romans 4:12), as was expressed by Paul of Tarsus. The very people that received from God the commandment 'Thou shalt not kill', itself experienced in a special measure what is meant by killing. It is not permissible for anyone to pass by this inscription with indifference.

And one inscription more, a chosen one, the plaque in the Russian language. I don't add any comment. We know which nation the inscription is about. We know about their participation in the last terrible war for the freedom of peoples. Also, this inscription we should not pass with indifference.

Finally, the last inscription: that in Polish. Six million Poles lost their lives during the Second World War: a fifth of the nation. Yet another stage in the centuries-old fight of this nation, my nation, for its fundamental rights among the peoples of Europe. Yet another loud cry for the right to a place of its own on the map of Europe. Yet another painful reckoning with the conscience of mankind.

(John Paul II, Mass at the Concentration Camp in Auschwitz, 7 June 1979)

Yesterday, Pope Francis sat silently in the cell of St Maximilian Kolbe, a Franciscan priest who took the place of another and died as a martyr in the starvation bunker in Auschwitz. The scenes of the pope sitting in prayer in the darkness of Kolbe's cell evokes for all of us the words of Jesus Christ from John's Gospel 'No greater love can anyone have than to lay down their lives for their friends' (John 15:13).

I see Fr Jacques Hamel's face here too. An elderly priest who spent his whole life until the end in the service of the Gospel. He was murdered and martyred in his church in Saint-Étienne-du-Rouvray, France, where he broke open the Word of God for the people and celebrated the Eucharist. Truly he shared in Jesus Christ's passion, death, and resurrection that morning last week.

In a world where we need to draw strength from the merciful heart of Jesus Christ, we pray that this same merciful heart will take away from those bent on evil and destruction their hearts of stone and give them hearts of flesh instead. We are fortified by the enthusiasm of so many young people who this night will pray in vigil with our Holy Father, Pope Francis, and will celebrate the Eucharist, the Mass, with him tomorrow in Krakow. We don't forget the many people in the face of evil and bloodshed who try to assist and help to heal wounds and dry the tears. We pray for peace with justice for all, and especially for the most vulnerable. St John Paul II, pray for us.

St Faustina, pray for us.

St Francis of Assisi, pray for us. Amen.

St Clare of Assisi

Sometimes, when we look at drawings or images of medieval saints, we could be fooled into thinking that perhaps, because he was a monk or she was a nun, they are pious or gentle or easily fooled. In many cases that couldn't be further from the truth. They were recognised for holiness, but they were tough and were no pushovers. Many of them suffered, denied themselves food and sleep, others lived in solitude, and others still were martyred. They were looked up to and relied upon by many, and they had a wise word and a prayer for most people. They were also well able to be honest and some could shoot from the hip at the risk of being unpopular. St Clare of Assisi was one such woman. By the end of her life, bishops and even a pope came around to her way of thinking.

Chiara Offreduccio was born into a noble family in Assisi on 16 July 1194. Her father was Favarone Sciffi, Count of Sasso-Rosso, and her mother was Ortolana. From a young age it was assumed that Clare was to marry in line with family tradition but, at 18 years old, she heard Francis of Assisi preaching and asked him if she could follow him and live after the manner of the Gospel. In March 1212, Francis received her into the order and placed her into the care of the Benedictine nuns of San Paolo. Her father made great efforts to get her to get out of the cloister and leave the order. Later she moved into a small church at San Damiano where she and her sisters stayed. They soon became known as the Poor Ladies of San Damiano and they lived a life of poverty and enclosure according to a rule given them by St Francis of Assisi. For Clare this vow of poverty was something that was non-negotiable. It was called the 'Privilegium Pauperitatis', which meant that the Poor Ladies guarded this grace to live in absolute poverty without possessions.

As a way of guarding the life they had chosen, a Roman Cardinal, Hugolino, was appointed 'protector' of the order. He later became Pope Gregory IX. As pope, he visited the Poor Ladies and was concerned about their living such a hard and austere life; he suggested relaxing the vow to live this privilege of poverty. Clare was a tough lady and was having none of it. For her and her sisters, poverty was just that, a privilege, which, well lived, freed them from distractions in order to focus on following Jesus Christ.

Francis of Assisi guided the order until he died in 1226 and after his death, Clare became Abbess of San Damiano. She took Francis's spirit as a good benchmark for the living of the religious life with her sisters in poverty and enclosure, and she fought off any attempt by church leaders to dispense her and the sisters from it. In 1224 the army of Frederick II came to plunder Assisi and the story goes that Clare came out of the enclosure and faced the emperor down by holding the monstrance with the Blessed Sacrament in her hands. The sight of this tenacious woman standing up to the emperor was enough to scare him so much that the army fled, terrified, without harming anyone in the city.

On 9 August 1253, Pope Innocent IV, in a papal Bull, a document given to Clare called 'Solet Annuere' confirmed that her rule would serve as the governing rule for the Poor Ladies' way of life. Never would anyone in the future be in danger of watering down the rule of the Poor Clares. Clare died two days later on 11 August; she was 59 years old. She was canonised on 26 September 1255. In 1958 Pope Pius XII named St Clare patron saint of television.

Batman Ben Farrell

I got to know Alan and Valerie Farrell and their second son, Jack, along with their family, a few years ago when they contacted me for prayers for Ben, their older boy who was batting childhood cancer. They fought that battle every step of the way with him, even crossing the Atlantic Ocean over to the USA for treatment for him. His story made the news and his heroic battle impressed many, including the Dublin Gaelic Football team and Jonathan Rhys Meyers among others. Sadly, his earthly healing was not to be. Today, his mam and dad continue his great legacy and I wanted to include the homily I gave at his funeral Mass. Valerie and Alan are happy for me to include this in the book in tribute to this great boy.

The saintly English King, Edward the Confessor, seeing how upset his friends were as he lay on his deathbed, consoled them all by saying; 'Don't be afraid, I'm going from the land of the dying into the land of the living.'

There was something other-worldly about Ben. From early on this lad was different – mature beyond his very young years. Alan and Val, you did so much, and you and the family fought so hard. You and the wonderful medics and nurses and carers on both sides of the Atlantic. You can be confident that you did as much as you could for him. Yet, you said it seemed that it was Ben who was taking care of you.

In Michigan, Valerie said, 'I wish I could take your pain for you.' Ben said, 'No, mammy, I wouldn't want to give it to you – I can handle it.' There's not a mother anywhere or a father who wouldn't swap places in a heartbeat with a sick child. And every dad and mam, and nana and granddad, feels the pain of a child and walks it every step of the way. Ben could handle it because he comes from good stock. You made him what he is and was.

And in truth he was a superhero. He battled hard with the cancer, yet the small boy of five years of age had the power of Ali, or Brogan, or Robbie Keane or Cluxton, and we feel his power now.

Whether it was singing 'Show me the way to go home' out loud in the hospital and banging out the beat on the table – his favourite movie was *Jaws*. It was like Brody, Hooper and Quint singing on Quint's boat the *Orca* after their tea. Or singing an Oasis number with his dad Alan in the van. Or building another Lego empire, sometimes the trips to buy a sneaky box of Lego (hiding it behind his back with that cheeky smile).

Or whether it was Batman. You know, superheroes don't hang around. They are always at the service of others. Just when we get to know Bruce Wayne the bat phone rings, and Wayne dons the bat suit and he's gone. They are too big for our world. And Perhaps Ben was too much of a force of nature for Planet Earth.

When the rest of us are struggling to stay young – Batman Ben lives forever young.

There's no answer as to why this had to happen. But maybe we get a glimpse of the next world when we open our eyes, and not necessarily with our eyesight but with our insight. We see more clearly in here. And our faith, the faith what was given to us by our parents and their parents helps us to see in the dark. Faith lights up the dark. Ben is gone to heaven, there is no doubt about that, and we will see him again. You will see Ben again, Val, and Alan, and Jack; down the road.

But you can connect with him any time in Jesus Christ who loves us. And this connection point is more powerful than any superfast

WiFi. And the signal never drops. But if I know Batman Ben, and you know him best, I wouldn't be at all surprised if you feel his power first, because he's praying for you now. In the words of Chief Brody, 'We're gonna need a bigger boat.'[1]

1   Included with the kind permission of Ben's parents, Valerie and Alan.

Jesus Christ is Risen

A MESSAGE OF HOPE. A HOMILY FOR EASTER SUNDAY

When the senior pupils of both schools come to Mass, I usually take some questions at the end of the session after Mass. They like to ask questions perhaps because it inevitably delays their having to go back to class. One of the pupils who recently made their confirmation in the last month asked me a very difficult question, 'Why did the nuns kill all the babies in Tuam?'

Before I tell you how I answered this, let me tell you that in Ireland, the church has been really under the cosh. It's been hard to be a minister of the Gospel today. I've felt it, the other friars have felt it, and my colleagues in ministry, religious and laity, have felt it. It's as if, once again, the historical institutional Church is making a spectacular success of scoring own goals. I'm not looking for sympathy either because most people in the real world have their own struggles; family, relationships, financial, illness and bereavement.

I saw a post on social media to do with the relaxation of the licensing laws on Good Friday. It read something like 'the pointy-hat brigade is slowly losing their grip' accompanied by a picture of a pint of Guinness. A few days later, I met a neighbour on Jervis Street who was delighted to show me a picture of himself drinking a pint on Good Friday, smiling at his act of defiance.

Will there soon be an end to the playing of the Angelus on RTÉ Radio and Television? There has been a call for the ending of the saying of the prayer at the beginning of the Dáil session each day. Could some of our sports stadia and playing pitches be renamed after a beverage company since some of them are currently named after catholic figures like Archbishop Croke? Then there's a whole other debate about Christian feasts and celebrating our national patron.

Across the world, we are seeing the dreadful scenes of children gassed in Syria, and in September 2015, we gazed in horror at the lifeless body of little Alan Kurdi washed up on the beaches of Bodrum, Turkey. Last week, many Coptic Christians were killed in an attack in Egypt and we remember the lines of Christian martyrs being killed on beaches by militant Islamists. We also hear that the cause for the beatification of Fr Jacques Hamel, martyred in 2016, in Saint-Étienne-du-Rouvray, has begun. All over the place, in great and small ways, ordinary people are suffering dreadfully and it's impossible to make sense of it all. We are hearing of people suffering day after day because of their faith in Jesus Christ.

Still, it's ordinary people who are making a difference all the time. Ordinary people's kindness to us here in the parish. Ordinary good people who don't take a blind bit of notice of what the papers may say. People who still come to Mass here. People who will cross the world to bring their new baby living in a new country back to have it baptised in the parish where they grew up. People who come in numbers to the Novena of Grace. People who always return to remember a loved one on their anniversary or their month's mind. People who kindly invite me to bless a house or a Garden of Remembrance, or to say a prayer over the mortal remains of a deceased nana or mammy laid out in their home. This is how we know Jesus Christ is alive. This is how we know Good Friday gives way to Easter Sunday. And maybe we will lose the Angelus bells on the radio sooner or later, but we will still ring our church bell here and many other church bells will ring out too. Perhaps we might see the end of the prayer said at the start of the daily Dáil session. There will be further efforts at bringing about the secularisation of the public square too because we are at the end of Christendom here in Ireland. Christendom is the political, economic and social order of our nation inspired by the Gospel ethic, and this is at an end. It is not the end of Christianity. Too many people have a deep faith in and love for Jesus Christ and this is thanks to the parents and grandparents we love who gave us the best years of their lives. We believe in Jesus Christ because of their faith.

Finally, I answered that lad's question; a powerful question, by saying the nuns didn't kill the babies in Tuam. There were indeed bad priests, and brothers and nuns. But there were and are many more kind and generous ones like Sr Consilio, Sr Stan, Fr Peter McVerry, Br Kevin, many hard-working parish clergy; the list goes on. These have a track record of beginning what we now know as the homeless services, the social housing services and addiction services today. And they are not the only ones. They are assisted by generous volunteers, many of them young people, who roll up their sleeves day and night to help those who are homeless. In 40 years' time, in a different Ireland, when another government calls the very few religious congregations to account for how they tried to help homeless families in the second decade of the 21st century, this will be our answer.

Jesus Christ is risen, and the message of the Gospel is and always will be a message of hope for all the world. Amen.

Pope John Paul II

I believe that John Paul II had a huge influence on my life and on my choice to join the Capuchin Order in 1987. Vocations are not an overnight thing, and there are no flashes of light and apparitions. The call to religious life and priesthood is normal and home grown and comes to fruition in God's time. All Jesus Christ asks is for an open heart

I grew up in a normal family in suburban Dublin and went to school in the 1970s and 1980s. We went to Sunday Mass and for a while, as a nine-year-old, I was a junior member of the Legion of Mary. Before my parents got married, they had been members of the Legion of Mary themselves and indeed many young people of their generation met and socialised in the Legion. My dad's first cousin, Brendan Shortall, had been a Legion of Mary envoy to Tanzania when he was a young man. In the Legion of Mary we used to meet on Tuesday evenings in Benedicta House on the South Circular Road. One of the things I remember well about the room we met in was that there was a life-sized poster of Pope John Paul II, who had only been elected within the last year. Frank Duff, the founder of the Legion of Mary, died in November 1980, and I remember my father went to the funeral.

I was born in 1969 in the pontificate of Pope St Paul VI. He died in 1978 and, apart from hearing his name being read out at Mass, I had no real idea about who he was. While I was familiar with the priests who were in my parish, I didn't know much about the church beyond our parish. I can recall the public surprise and shock at the death of Pope John Paul I only 30 days after his election, and I remember the news coming through on RTÉ television. I know now, apart from the sadness of the death of 'the smiling pope', who came as cardinal from Venice, it was going to be a logistical nightmare to organise a second autumn conclave in Rome. And so, on 16 October 1978, the day before my ninth birthday, 58-year-old Cardinal Karol Josef Wojtyla, the Archbishop of Krakow, was elected pope, taking the name John Paul II. I remember the huge excitement of this election and the media reports that he was the first non-Italian pope in over 400 years. He was the first Slavic pope and a pope from a country behind the 'Iron Curtain'. I began to hear the priest say, 'John Paul, our pope, and Dermot, our bishop', each Sunday at Mass. I was in fourth class at school in CBS James's Street, and soon we started to see pictures and portraits of Pope John Paul II in school and in the church.

I don't recall any of the details of the preparations for the visit of Pope John Paul to Ireland. I do, however, remember a letter the pope wrote to the Church in Ireland on the weekend before his arrival which was published in the *Sunday Press* together with a full-colour picture of his recent visit to Poland.

Pope John Paul and his party landed in Dublin airport on Saturday, 29 September 1979. Being aeroplane mad, I knew that he flew to Ireland on board an Aer Lingus Boeing 747 named *St Patrick*. This was unusual in that Alitalia generally gets to fly the pope outbound from Italy on his apostolic voyages. It has been a tradition for the Holy See to send a telegram of prayerful good wishes from the pope to every country he flies over.

I don't know where or when this was arranged, but I remember there was an 'alarm car' driving around the streets of the area we lived in and it was designed to wake us up in time to get to the parish church and to walk on pilgrimage to the Phoenix Park. We were lucky as we lived at the time in Rialto, which was only about three kilometres from the Phoenix Park. Soon my mother, myself and my brother Kevin were arriving in the '15 acres' of the Phoenix Park, sporting our papal stickers with the location of the corral we were to go to. Along with our packed lunch and a flask of tea, we carried our 'papal stools', small collapsible canvas stools. I remember my mother sprayed fly and wasp repellent on our coats in case of wasp stings. And so, we settled in and waited for the pope to arrive. The choir, drawn from church choirs from all over the country, was rehearsing and people were looking towards the altar area, some through binoculars, across a sea of people.

There was great excitement when we were made aware of the approach of the papal plane, 'Sierra-India', *St Patrick*, on its way up the River Liffey, escorted by the Irish Air Corps. It turned right over the park on its way north to Dublin airport. We had to wait for another hour or so as there were formalities at the airport and the pope was then transported to the park by helicopters. This, too, was a great sight, as the chopper came in towards the west of the park and flew in a semi-circle to land at the back of the papal cross near the grounds of the American ambassador's residence. Eventually the entrance procession began and Frank Patterson and Bernadette Greevy led us in hymns and songs. The pope began the Mass in Irish and compared his desire to come to Ireland with the call of the Irish to St Patrick to come and minister to them.

In 1979 we didn't have the same technology available to us for mass gatherings like we do today. There were big grey tubular loudspeakers erected all over the park and the voices and singing boomed and echoed to all corners of the 15 acres and beyond. This was a time before big screens, so my memory of the pope was just a tiny white dot at the foot of the papal cross. Some people around me had binoculars so it was easier for them to see the pope and the archbishops of Armagh and Dublin alongside him.

The last memory I recall is of Pope John Paul being driven around in the popemobile. It was a converted van, painted yellow, with an open area where he could be seen as it moved through the crowds. I remember seeing it at a bit of a distance but still recall him in his red cloak as he waved to and blessed the cheering crowds. I remember shouting 'Pope John Paul!' at the top of my voice and I wonder did he hear me!

At home that afternoon, we watched Pope John Paul as he visited Drogheda in the Archdiocese of Armagh. Today, it is well known that it wasn't possible for the pope to travel into the North of Ireland due to the Troubles. In Drogheda, he was able to set foot in the ecclesiastical province of Ulster while not going over the border. In his address, he spoke directly to the men and women of violence. He said, 'Now I wish to speak to all men and women engaged in violence. I appeal to you, in language of passionate pleading. On my knees I beg you to turn away from the paths of violence and to return to the ways of peace. You may claim to seek justice. I too believe in justice and seek justice. But violence only delays the day of justice. Violence destroys the work of justice. Further violence in Ireland will only drag down to ruin the land you claim to love and the values you claim to cherish. In the name of God, I beg you: return to Christ, who died so that men might live in forgiveness and peace. He is waiting for you, longing for each one of you to come to him so that he may say to each of you: your sins are forgiven; go in peace.' (John Paul II Mass in Drogheda, 29 September 1979)

Later in the evening, we went down to my Nana's house near the city centre from where some of us walked up to Thomas Street to wait for the pope to pass by on his way to Áras an Uachtaráin. He was to come in the famous popemobile. Thomas Street is famous in Dublin's south city centre for markets and street trading. The motorcade came along with sirens and blue lights, and there was Pope John Paul II, flanked by Cardinal Tomás Ó Fiaich, Archbishop of Armagh, and Dermot Ryan, Archbishop of Dublin. I remember the pope in sweeping gestures blessing the crowds on both sides of Thomas Street in the shadow of the famous John's Lane Church. I think I recall my Nana saying something like 'Did we ever think we'd ever in our lives get to see the pope of Rome coming down Thomas Street?' For Irish Catholics of my Nana's generation, who were born in the infancy of the 20th century, popes were very far removed from the lives of ordinary Irish people. An audience with the pope was maybe then a once in a lifetime experience and then, if it did happen, it would be among thousands of people. When my grandparents were children, all Catholics would go down on one knee and kiss the ring of a bishop or a cardinal on the rare occasions they met one. So, when Paul VI and John Paul II began to travel to other countries, they brought the papacy out into the world. Paul, John Paul, Benedict, and now Francis, in the spirit of the Acts of the Apostles, travel 'to all nations' on pilgrimage to meet with the masses to spread the Gospel of Jesus Christ.

Pope John Paul travelled to Galway, Limerick, Clonmacnoise, and Maynooth during his weekend in Ireland. In Galway, the pope had a powerful encounter with young people. Here it was that John Paul told the young people of Ireland that he loved them. He received the now famous 11-minute standing ovation.

The goal of Pope John Paul's visit was to visit Knock Shrine. In August 1879, Our Blessed Lady, along with St John and St Joseph, appeared to several people at the gable end of the parish church in teeming rain. The apparition was powerfully Eucharistic as the Lamb on the altar was also visible. The pope came 100 years later as a pilgrim like Mary, to give hope to the people of Ireland. He presented a golden rose to the shrine and gave the church of Our Lady of Knock the status of basilica. Knock has a special relationship with pilgrims who are sick, and the ministry of Pope John Paul II has had a special outreach to those who were sick and suffering. Indeed, he himself was a patient several times during his long pontificate, not least after the May 1981 assassination attempt which left him very seriously injured. Pope John Paul II left Shannon Airport on Monday, 1 October 1979 and flew across the Atlantic Ocean bound for Boston where he was beginning an apostolic voyage to the USA. In his pontificate, from 1978 to 2005, he made more than 100 international trips, crossing the world with the Gospel message of Jesus Christ.

I have been hugely influenced by the papacy of John Paul II and many of my friends and people of my generation will remember him as perhaps the first 'superstar pope'. I was nearly 10 years of age when I saw him in the Phoenix Park and, while I knew some-thing about the pope, I hadn't any knowledge about hierarchies or the Holy See and all that type of thing. What I do remember of him is those sweeping gestures and the powerful voice and the huge buzz he created all over the country on that weekend in 1979. Over the years, I remember reports about him and news of him meet-ing people like President Reagan, Princess Diana, Queen Elizabeth, Mother Teresa of Calcutta and so on. I remember hearing stories of his sporting abilities and his fitness. He was a very accomplished skier and an experienced mountain climber, who loved to spend as much time as he could in the great outdoors.

For my generation, the news that came through on 13th May 1981 was a huge shock. During Pope John Paul's weekly audience, a Turkish gunman, Mehmet Ali Agca, shot the pope at point blank range as he was being driven around through the crowds. He was very seriously injured and was rushed immediately to the Gemelli hospital in Rome. Some pilgrims were also injured. Following the operation to save his life, he asked for prayers for his attacker who he had 'sincerely pardoned'. He recuperated for much of the summer of 1981 and, a year later, he made a trip to Fatima, where he placed a bullet from one of his wounds in the statue of Our Lady of Fatima. He profoundly believed that it was through the intercession of Our Lady of Fatima that his life was spared as the shooting happened on the Feast of Our Lady of Fatima. On 28 December 1983, Pope John Paul II visited Ali Agca in prison and the pictures of the encounter were beamed all across the world by the media covering the story.

In his later years, we saw Pope John Paul grow old and frail. The sweeping gestures of a youthful and fit churchman were replaced by slow and weak movements. In the Jubilee year 2000, we saw the pope struggling to move to the Holy Door in St Peter's and getting help in ceremonially pushing it open. Everywhere he went he needed the assistance of his aides and his secretary Archbishop Dziwisz. Towards the end of his life, he could hardly move, and many remember his last public appearance when he couldn't even talk. Again, I believe this points to his witness to the Gospel of life where he called on us to respect all human life from the moment of conception to the moment of natural death. He lived his witness of respect for the sick and those with disabilities in his own body as he got older and frailer. Pope John Paul's last illness and death were almost live on television all over the world. Television networks and satellite vans descended on Rome and on St Peter's Square as he neared the end. This man who captured the hearts of many people in the world and also provoked controversy among others in life, was dying on prime-time television. The next few weeks would be box-office viewing, with the papal funeral and the conclave that eventually elected Pope Benedict XVI. Pope John Paul II died on 2 April 2005, praying at the last, 'Let me go to the house of the Father.' His funeral was attended by many world leaders, including

President George W. Bush and Presidents George H.W. Bush and Bill Clinton, who knelt and prayed by his catafalque in St Peter's. The multitude gathered in St Peter's Square keeping vigil as he lay dying and through the following days and especially at the funeral kept calling out 'Santo Subito' (sainthood now). He was canonised along with Pope John XIII on 27 April 2014 – Divine Mercy Sunday.

I've said a lot about my memories of the pastoral visit of Pope John Paul II to Ireland in 1979 and included some other memories I've had of him. If someone was to ask me what is the one stand-out thing that John Paul II gave to the Church in his 27 years as pope, for me it would have to be his call to holiness. He was criticised for canonising too many saints and was accused of making sanctity easier. However, I think that's great, because we're all encouraged to aim high. Why shouldn't an ordinary person, woman or man, girl or boy, aspire to sainthood, and not only martyrs, nuns, monks, bishops and popes? We're all called to holiness, therefore we're all called to be saints. Who was it that said, 'the saint is the sinner who never stopped trying'?

One small regret I had was that I never got to meet Pope John Paul II personally. I know that meeting a pope is not something that's particularly easy to organise and to be fair to the pope, a lot of people want to meet him! I did try to apply to attend one of his daily private Masses in the Apostolic Palace in the early 2000s. I was told how to go about it and I was given the details of who to write to etc., and as I was going to be in Rome I said I'd give it a try. In fairness, someone from the Vatican rang the day before and unfortunately the pope had a public Mass the next day, so it wasn't to be. I have spoken to people, including clergy who have met John Paul II and I've been impressed, and a little bit jealous, to hear of their experiences and to hear how moved they've been to meet him. I remember speaking to some people who had the privilege of attending his morning Mass in the Apostolic Palace and hearing how powerful it was to just observe him in communion with Jesus Christ. One commented that one could almost see him bend under the weight of the Church on his shoulders.

Recently, a friend of mine, a fellow Franciscan, sent me a photo of myself and another Capuchin sitting listening to John Paul II speaking to us following the Mass of thanksgiving the day after he beatified Padre Pio in May 1999. On the Monday, Cardinal Sodano celebrated a Mass of thanksgiving and we got to concelebrate and after Mass we were told to wait on in the hot sun. We were not disappointed as the Holy Father came out to greet us and address us and my friend who was a concelebrant sitting in the row behind took a photo and there I am in the company of a saint. While I never got to meet him personally, I hope one day down the line I will. In the meantime, I will treasure that photo. Totus Tuus!

Scaffolding, Bricks and Mortar

We're getting the church painted by degrees. There has been ongoing restoration work done during my time as parish priest and before my time. Naturally, the cost of the work done has been great and we have developed ways for people to donate and contribute. We are one of the oldest churches in the diocese and, indeed, perhaps the oldest parish on the north side of the city. People from all over the world have contacted us for information about their ancestry. This, among other initiatives, helps us to continue to tip away with our restoration work.

In 2016, as we looked towards the bicentenary of the parish, 1817–2017, we began to paint the walls of the church, which were badly in need of cleaning and painting since the last time it was painted was 1991. Because the lower parts of the walls were quite marked and dirty, and because they were accessible with ladders, we painted them first. Before Christmas 2016 we painted the sanctuary; the high altar and the two side altars. A generous benefactor kindly offered to pay for this phase of the work which greatly helped us to plan for the third phase, which necessitates high scaffolding around the walls as we paint them all the way to the ceiling. Next year, please God, we will see about phase four; painting the ceiling itself.

So, at the moment we have scaffolding around the front of the sanctuary and all along the walls of the church. It is a tight squeeze to say Mass on the altar, although it's a small sacrifice as we look forward to the completion of this stage of the works. We look forward to the Archbishop of Dublin coming to celebrate our Mass of Thanksgiving on 25 August, the feast of St Michan, the patron of our parish.

I was sitting in the church for a short while the other day as Stephen and John were on the scaffolding painting. As I looked around at the scaffolding, I was reminded that, with its bars, and platforms, and its planks, and its pins and rivets, it just that, scaffolding. The scaffold helps us to look beyond and make things new. As it stands along the high walls of our church on this 200th year of its opening, it tells a story of faith not just over two centuries, but over the millennium since St Michan called a people together in the name of Jesus Christ. The scaffolding also reminds us of the story of our parish from Capel Street to Parkgate Street and from the north banks of the River Liffey at the Four Courts to Constitution Hill. It also tells us of a people who were born here in this parish and who now live in different countries and who are part of the Christian community all across the world.

The scaffolding assists us. It raises us to great heights safely and it helps us to see things in a new way. The faith story of the people of this parish down through the years is a scaffolding to support the parishioners of the future to carry the message. The scaffolding is helping us to paint and refurbish the walls of the church. And, indeed, the walls of the church are just bricks and mortar, but our church is more than that, it is family, it is community, it is young people, it is schools, it is neighbours, it is history. Its heart beats with stories and prayers, and its blood courses through the very soul of the people here.

John the Baptist

MAKING NOISE

John the Baptist was languishing in a prison cell, having been put there by Herod because he strongly disagreed with Herod's marriage to Herodias, who was already married to Herod's brother Philip (and Philip was still alive). Sounds like this could be the subject line of a daytime reality television show.

From the beginning, even in his mother's womb, John was making noise about Jesus Christ (Luke 1:41). When next we see John in action, he is in the Jordan River, baptising all who wish to turn from their sinful ways and begin again (Luke 3ff). Ultimately, he calls people's attention to the presence of Christ. 'Behold the Lamb of God who takes away the sin of the world ... ' (John 1:29).

John is a noisemaker, therefore, and while Herod is irritated by the things John says, he is intrigued at the same time, since John is a very powerful preacher and holy man. Herodias on the other hand, is not impressed and endeavours to stop the noise and to cut the power.

Each of us contends with noise each day with every sound demanding our attention. Generally, we pick and choose which one is the winner. Unpleasant feelings can take a lot of our attention and the worse we feel, the noisier it gets, and our minds and spirit are filled with negativity. So, we need to hear a new sound and to turn up the volume of positivity and joy. This way we crowd out the negative, giving it no more room. A powerful way to do this is to do good things and to practise charity and kindness. With time, we only have room for the good and pleasant things in our heads and lives and spirit.

Herodias's daughter is asked to dance for the king's party guests and is publicly promised anything she wants, even up to 'half of his Kingdom'. Herodias goes to her mother and asks her for advice. Herodias wastes no time in advising her to ask the king to give her the head of John the Baptist on a silver platter. The king accedes to the request – he must, to keep his promise.

Does this silence John the Baptist? No. The proclamation of the good news of the Gospel continues from the Kingdom of Heaven. The joyful noise of the message of Jesus Christ cannot be silenced.

Give me Joy in my Heart[2]

We have to make our minds up to be joyful. It comes down to a choice; do we stand out in the sunshine or do we prefer to stay indoors with the curtains closed? It is easier said than done, depending on what kind of form we are in. Negative thinking saps our energy and closes us in on ourselves. And it is harder these days to avoid the onslaught of bad news and even aggression out there.

Most of us have profiles on social media. Priests and religious are to be found on Facebook, Twitter, Instagram and LinkedIn. I know there are those who prefer to avoid it like the plague, and maybe that is smart, but there are bishops who regularly post pastoral initiatives and photos on their Facebook and Twitter accounts. Even the Holy Father posts on Twitter in several languages daily to approximately 40 million people.

A friend is recovering from neurosurgery. He's finishing a course of radium treatment and is doing well, thank God. When he began to show symptoms, he went to his GP and, because it was ahead of a bank holiday weekend, he couldn't get an early appointment with this particular specialist. He was in a lot of pain, so he looked up some prominent neurosurgeons on LinkedIn and he saw the profile page for the specialist. He sent off a message to him and by return he had a reply and was given an appointment for a consultation on the Tuesday. He told me that the specialist asked him what the symptoms were etc., and an MRI was arranged very quickly. The

2   Paper given to diocesan clergy – October 2017.

benefits of having a LinkedIn account. The world has got smaller as a result of all of the above and while there are dangers and pitfalls within social media, they reflect the dangers we all face in our lives.

The country is recovering from Storm Ophelia. Last weekend we were updated minute by minute by the mainstream media and social media about the track of this ex-hurricane. It was historic, as hurricanes originate somewhere in the vicinity of the Azores and track in a westerly direction. However, this one got caught in a jetstream and began to track north-east towards the south-western coast of Ireland. We all know what happened, but we were well-prepared largely due to people sharing information on social media. While it was bad news that this storm was barrelling towards Ireland, more positively for example, there were television updates and even the RTÉ Radio presenters on Monday morning went wall-to-wall with news about the storm and its track. Via social media people were opening their homes to rough sleepers. Gyms and halls, hotels and guesthouses were offering help. Brother Kevin had 102 rough sleepers on the floor of the Day Centre during Monday afternoon and overnight.

In the last 12 months we have seen terrible atrocities from around the world coming into our living rooms and onto our smartphones. The attack on Manchester at the Ariana Grande concert. The car ploughing into pedestrians in London. The van crashing into people, including children, in Las Ramblas in Barcelona. The evil of a man shooting a rifle at people from a hotel room window in Las Vegas. Yet, in the midst of these evil acts of violence, ordinary people do extraordinary acts of love. Again, we see people queueing to donate blood. Taxi drivers turning off their machines to get people home safely, free of charge. People going on social media and offering a room or lodgings for anyone caught up in the violence. Social media sites themselves setting up pages to offer a place for people to register as safe. In the midst of what is darkness there are specks of light, which gives great hope.

Back in September, Pope Francis had this advice at his general audience:

> Do not surrender to the night; remember that the
> first enemy to conquer is not outside: it is within you.
> Therefore, do not give space to bitter, obscure thoughts.
> This world is the first miracle God made. God has placed
> the grace of new wonders in our hands. Faith and hope go
> forward together. Believe in the existence of the loftiest
> and most beautiful truths. Trust in God the Creator, in
> the Holy Spirit who moves everything towards the good,
> in the embrace of Christ who awaits every man and
> woman at the end of their life. Believe, he awaits you. The
> world walks thanks to the gaze of many men and women
> who have opened up breaches, who have built bridges,
> who have dreamed and believed, even when they heard
> derisive words around them.
> Wherever you may be, build! If you are down, stand up!
> Never stay down; stand up, allow yourself to be helped to
> stand up. If you are seated, set out on a journey! If bore-
> dom paralyses you, banish it with good works! If you feel
> empty or demoralised, ask that the Holy Spirit may fill
> your emptiness anew ... (Pope Francis. General Audience
> Wednesday, 20 September 2017 www.vatican.va)

He's spot-on. We are called to be people of Hope. In an Angelus address in Australia in 1986, Saint Pope John Paul II said:

> We do not pretend that life is all beauty. We are aware
> of darkness and sin, of poverty and pain. But we know
> Jesus has conquered sin and passed through his own

pain to the glory of the Resurrection. And we live in the light of his Paschal Mystery – the mystery of his Death and Resurrection. 'We are an Easter People and Alleluia is our song! (www.vatican.va)

It is hard to focus on this when at times there is no escape from the bad news and the bad weather. But if I can't find a way out and if I feel like I'm smothered by all this, then I've got to reach out. I need others. We need each other and I'm lucky because I'm part of a religious order and so from day one I was accepted as a brother and I live in community. Now, I'm not going to lie, sometimes I envy you guys living on your own. And to be fair, the other fellows that live with me probably find me hard to live with at times. I remember when I was a student one of the older friars was grumbling at us because he couldn't hear the 9 o'clock news and he shouted; 'Grrrr! ye harriers!' ('Harriers' was the name the older friars gave to the student friars in temporary profession before we made our final vows.) Quick as a flash, one of the lads said; 'We are the fruits of all the prayers ye said for vocations!'

So, we've got to reach out. I couldn't do what I am doing without going for regular spiritual direction and also pastoral supervision. I was perpetually professed as a Capuchin friar in 1994 and I was ordained priest in 1997. I've been in school chaplaincy, local leadership in two of our friaries, I've been on our Provincial Leadership team, and I've been in hospital chaplaincy in Beaumont. Right now, I'm parish priest in Halston Street, near the Four Courts, a parish in the care of the Capuchins since 1983. While I was chaplain in Beaumont, I began to go for supervision, and it was one of the best decisions I made. I found hospital ministry very challenging, and working in that environment, with emergencies, sickness and death, over a 12-hour shift either at night or during the day, isn't easy. I remember one night being on duty from 8pm to 8am and during the night seven people died. Going from one family to the other over the night for anointing and prayers was very hard. Yet many of them were concerned about me. 'It must be very hard for you, Father.' I will always be grateful for my time in Beaumont Hospital where I learned so much and where no matter who came through the emergency department, bad or good, all were triaged and treated. I salute the skills of our nursing, medical and care staff. So, I'm lucky enough to be in ministry, and if there's any place where we are challenged to keep the highest standards it is in ministry today. We minister in the name of Jesus Christ and his Church.

Being in religious life and in the priesthood is a great joy. I would say the challenge for me is to balance ministry with the administration of the parish. Thank God we have good personnel and Archbishop Martin has set up good diocesan offices and an excellent HR office which greatly helps us in running the machinery of the parish. I tend to switch off when there's talk of finance and paperwork. So, I try to concentrate on the ministry side, the people side.

St Michan's Parish is situated in the heart of the fruit and vegetable markets, so many of the Moore Street dealers live in the parish and many of them come regularly to Mass. They are a tonic to talk to and deeply generous people. The church is 200 years old this year and one of the things we did as a parish in preparation for the Mass of thanksgiving on 25 August, the Feast of St Michan, was to go out to the different parts of the parish to bless homes and families. The people in many ways took over. They put up bunting, they put out little altars and we had hospitality after the prayers. I told the archbishop at the Mass: there isn't a house that isn't blessed in this parish! Ten of us did the Camino in September again as part of the bicentenary of the parish church. We look forward to the annual Mass of remembrance in November which we say down in the old

Fruit Markets building where they decorate the altar with flowers, fruit and vegetables.

I get great life in identifying times and occasions of encounter with the people. In many cases this is through the celebration of the Sacraments. This gives me hope when I begin to pay attention to the attacks on the Church and our Catholic life out there. As I said at the top of this talk, it's hard to avoid. We are called to be joyful ministers of the Gospel, and in his Holy Thursday Chrism Mass homily in 2014 Pope Francis spoke about the grace of the Sacrament of Holy Orders as a source of joy for the priest himself and for the people we serve; and it reflects the generosity of God for us and in us.

> 'For me, there are three significant features of our priestly joy. It is a joy which anoints us (not one which 'greases' us, making us unctuous, sumptuous and presumptuous), it is a joy which is imperishable and it is a missionary joy which spreads and attracts, starting backwards – with those farthest away from us.' (Pope Francis, Holy Thursday 2014, www.vatican.va)

Pope Francis says that joy anoints, in that Grace fills us to the brim and overflows, fully, abundantly and entirely in each priest. We are anointed down to our very bones ... and our joy, which wells up from deep within, is the echo of this anointing. It has been there from the start and we need to remember to tap into it in prayer especially in the Scriptures and before the Blessed Sacrament.

He explains that it is imperishable, in that the fullness of the Gift, which no one can take away or increase, is an unfailing source of joy: an imperishable joy which the Lord has promised no one can take from us (John 16:22).

Pope Francis continues that it is missionary, in that priestly joy is deeply bound up with God's holy and faithful people, for it is an eminently missionary joy. Our anointing is meant for anointing God's holy and faithful people: for baptising and confirming them, healing and sanctifying them, blessing, comforting and evangelising them.

I touched on prayer there. And that is the danger for us – whether in religious life and or priestly ministry – we just touch on prayer. Twenty years ago, one of our late great friars, now gone home to God, spotted something in the *Sunday Independent* one morning after Mass. It was about a well-known priest at the time and he had made the news in some area of pastoral activity, and I think the headline was 'Popular Priest ... '. And he was off. 'Popular Priest, what does he mean Popular Priest?', 'Oh, he's great with the youth', 'Father such-a-body gives a great homily.' 'Years ago we had golden priests and wooden chalices,' he lamented. 'Now we have golden chalices and wooden priests ... what we want are holy priests.'

And he was right. We need to rediscover our call to holiness and, of course, this is about the whole self, mind, body and spirit. The holiest men I know and knew in the order were kind, prayerful, approachable, available, accountable, transparent and obedient. That didn't mean they didn't have their moments; look at St Padre Pio – friars often had to be on hand to meet upset penitents when he ran them from the confession boxes. But they were holy men, they were deeply prayerful in a down-to-earth way and holy through and through. One of them wasn't much of a preacher and he'd carry a load of books into the ambo with him and he'd stumble right through the homily, but he was so kind and caring to those who were in trouble or any need. He had a real empathy for the bereaved and a great ministry to the dying. He never had a minute and I remember when he got his first mobile phone he was tormented.

Another man who I judge as holy was a former provincial minister, now gone to God. He was provincial in the aftermath of the Second Vatican Council. If there was ever a man who blessed the order it was him. A missionary, home from Zambia, an Irish Capuchin but a native of the U., told me the story of asking for holidays to see his family in north-west England. In those days they got home to Ireland for six months every six years. He went to the previous provincial in Church Street and asked could he go on to visit his family in the UK and it was 'Let me think about it'. Then he got an answer after dinner; 'OK – go to England but be back on Friday' (and this was Tuesday). So he travelled on Wednesday, had Thursday with his mother, and back to Ireland on Friday. Horrible. Years later, the next provincial apologised for the way he had been previously treated and told him to go and spend as long as he needed and see his family. At his funeral in the early 2000s the Capuchin friar who preached said this provincial minister was 'Our Pope John'.

Finally, a word from the writings of St Francis of Assisi about priests and the friars who are priests. He sets the bar very high when he speaks of priesthood. He had an enormous respect for the priesthood. He wasn't a priest himself as he felt genuinely unworthy of it, although we know he was a deacon because in the sources we see him minister as a deacon in the story of the first Christmas crib at Greccio. We also know he was a cleric because he speaks of 'we' who are clerics. He accepted diaconate also because he was minister general of the order.

From the Testament of St Francis of Assisi, we read:

> Afterwards the Lord gave me and still gives me such faith in priests who live according to the manner of the holy Roman Church because of their order, that if they were to persecute me, I would still have recourse to them. And if I possessed as much wisdom as Solomon had and I came upon pitiful priests of this world, I would not preach contrary to their will in the parishes in which they live.

And I desire to fear, love and honour them and all
others as my masters. And I do not wish to consider sin
in them because I discern the Son of God in them and
they are my masters. And I act in this way since I see
nothing corporally of the Most High Son of God in this
world except His Most Holy Body and Blood which they
receive and which they alone administer to others ...

In the Letter to the Entire Order, St Francis addresses the friars
who are priests and reminds them of their high calling. Eight hundred years later, aside from the kind of language that was used at the
time, these are still wise words and images for us.

See your dignity, 'friar' (cf.. 1 Corinthians 1:26) priests,
and be holy, because He himself is Holy (cf Leviticus
19:2). And just as beyond all others on account of this
ministry the Lord God has honoured you, so even you
are to love, revere, and honour Him beyond all others.
Great miseries and miserable infirmity, when you hold
Him so near and you care for anything else in the whole
world. Let the whole of mankind tremble with fear,
let the whole world begin to tremble, and let heaven
exult, when there is upon the Altar in the hand of the
priest 'Christ, the Son of the living God' (John 11:27)!
O admirable height and stupendous esteem! O sublime
humility! O humble sublimity, which the Lord of the
universe, God and the Son of God, so humbles Himself;
that for our salvation hides himself under the little
form of bread! See, friars, the humility of God and 'pour
out your hearts before Him' (Psalm 61:9); humble even
yourselves, so that you may be exalted by Him (cf.. 1
Peter 5:6; James 4:10). Therefore, hold back nothing of

yourselves for yourselves, so that He may receive you totally, because He gives Himself totally to you.

I would argue that St Francis would urge all of us to be joyful ministers of the Gospel for our time, a time which is understanding priesthood, celibacy and a lifelong commitment less and less.

I also point to Francis of Assisi who shows us an example of humility, moderation, minority, poverty, non-violence and beauty on the inside, in a world today with much anger, aggression, excess, selfishness and 'I'.

In the 21st century the world still holds up Francis of Assisi, who died in 1226; our present pope took his name. It seems to me that Francis of Assisi's values are things that the world needs more and more. But this is the thing of it; Francis of Assisi always points to Jesus Christ. I'll leave you with the first Chapter of the Rule of Saint Francis of Assisi:

> This is the rule and life of the Friars Minor, namely, to observe the holy Gospel of our Lord Jesus Christ by living in obedience, in poverty and in chastity. Brother Francis promises obedience and reverence to Pope Honorius and to his successors who shall be canonically elected, and to the Roman Church. The other brothers are bound to obey Brother Francis, and his successors.

Salvator Mundi – No Change

This has been a week where homeless agencies in Ireland are under severe pressure to continue to help what seems to be a growing crisis among homeless families and rough sleepers. We have seen genuine concern from smaller homeless services, voluntary groups who bring hot soup and basics around to those sleeping rough in the city each night, following comments in the media saying that this isn't always helpful in the main. The problem is perennial but now in wintertime we see the crisis deepen here.

It has been a week when we have seen Bob Geldof giving back his Honorary Freedom of Dublin City because he feels in conscience that he can't share the same roll of honour as Aung San Suu Kyi. U2 have also expressed criticism of her on their website; ' ... the violence and terror being visited on the Rohingya people are appalling atrocities and must stop. Aung San Suu Kyi's silence is starting to look a lot like assent ... '. The pictures on our television screens of these suffering people are harrowing.

We are also seeing terrible scenes of suffering in Yemen and the BBC reports online today that more than 7,600 people have been killed and 42,000 injured since March 2015. Again, our television screens show the massive suffering of innocent men, women and children and Yemen is on the brink of famine.

In New York a painting of Christ by Leonardo da Vinci, *Salvator Mundi*, has been sold at auction for 450 million dollars. It has been sold to an anonymous bidder and therefore we don't know if it will emerge some day for people to see and view. There aren't too many people who would be able to stump up that kind of cash to buy a painting by da Vinci, I would imagine. And if it was a private collector, who will get to see it again? At least the big museums of the world would afford people the chance to see this and perhaps time will tell.

I was thinking about this after I saw a tweet the other day from Fr Paddy Byrne (@frpaddybyrne), (who wrote the book *All Will Be Well* published by Columba Books). He said 'We can all have a personal life saving friendship with the person this image depicts ... for free ... '. I totally agree with this. A life-saving relationship with Jesus Christ fuels all of us to endeavour to make a difference in people's lives. It spurs people like Sr Consilio, Sr Stan, Fr Peter McVerry, Br Kevin and others to help the homeless and those in addiction as they have been doing since the 1960s and 1970s. It inspires people, and many of them young professionals – nurses, medics, surgeons, therapists, engineers, social workers, teachers etc. – to give up some years of their lives to travel with NGOs, the Red Cross, the Red Crescent and MSF, for example, to areas broken by war, disease and famine. And of course, I am conscious that those who may belong to another faith community and also those who don't believe in God, still work tirelessly to make the world a better place.

Pope Francis has inaugurated this Sunday as the first World Day of the Poor. In his message about this he says; 'I invite the whole Church, and men and women of good will everywhere, to turn their gaze on this day to all those who stretch out their hands and plead for our help and solidarity. They are our brothers and sisters, created and loved by the one Heavenly Father.' (Pope Francis. First World Day of the Poor. www.vatican.va)

We keep in our hearts all who are broken by homelessness, violence, poverty and famine, caught in the crossfire of selfishness among those who want more and more at the expense of the most vulnerable. The happiest people are those who are at the service of others.

Padre Pio as a Capuchin Friar

Padre Pio was asked once, 'Who are you?' He replied; 'I'm just a poor friar who prays.' I've no doubt that he would prefer to be remembered for this rather than all his supernatural gifts. Many years ago, one of our Irish Capuchins, who ran the Padre Pio Prayer Group in Church Street, often said of Padre Pio that he will not be canonised because of the stigmata, or the bi-location, or the ability to read souls, or the supernatural gifts he had. Padre Pio will be canonised because of how he lived the Franciscan life.

We know that Padre Pio was born Francesco Forgione into a farming family in 1887 in Pietrelcina in south-eastern Italy. Interestingly, this man who would become a Capuchin Franciscan and eventually bear the stigmata was given the same name as the great saint of Italy, Francis of Assisi, who also bore the stigmata in his time. While Francesco Forgione didn't have great health as a boy and as a young man, he did like to play the odd game of football with his friends in the locality. Religion and the Church had a big part to play in everyone's life then and Francesco was no exception. It was felt by many people who knew the Forgiones that Francesco would probably end up as a priest and a religious. He was drawn to the Capuchins because he was inspired by a talk he heard from a young Capuchin brother who was questing in the area. Capuchin friars often travelled between friaries preaching and promoting vocations and questing – or begging for alms for the friary and the poor.

When he joined the Capuchins in his late teens in Morcone, 20 kilometres to the north of Pietrelcina at the turn of the 20th Century, as a novice friar he was given the name Brother Pio. In those days the Capuchin friars were identified more by the place they came from than by their surname (Padre Pio of Pietrelcina rather than Padre Pio Forgione). As a student friar in simple (or temporary) vows he was in studies for the priesthood. He was perpetually professed, and then ordained to the priesthood in the Cathedral of Benevento on 10 August 1910 at the age of 23. Four days later he offered his first Mass. Interestingly, for six years he was permitted to remain with his family living at home as a Capuchin due to continued bad health. It was after this, on 4 September 1916, that he was sent by his superiors to be stationed in the friary of Our Lady of Graces, San Giovanni Rotondo, in the province of Foggia. Apart from a period of military service in the Medical Corps in Naples in 1915, Padre Pio was to remain in San Giovanni Rotondo until his death in 1968.

All Capuchin Franciscans take the vows of obedience, poverty and chastity. We take them for a probationary period of time first. Later, after discernment by the student friar, those responsible for formation and the Holy Spirit, we take that lifelong commitment. In the first chapter of the rule of St Francis of Assisi, which was approved by the Holy See in 1223, we read: 'This is the rule and life of the Friars Minor, namely to observe the Holy Gospel of Our Lord Jesus Christ, living in obedience, without anything of one's own, and in chastity. Brother Francis promises obedience and reverence to our lord Pope Honorius and all his successors canonically elected, and to the Roman Church. And all the friars are bound to obey Brother Francis and his successors.' Here we see the beginning of the rule of life that Brother Pio professed and he did so living in community with the other brothers.

Day in and day out, and sometimes rising at midnight, Padre Pio lived the rule of the friars. They had meditation in common and prayed the liturgical hours during the day. The friar's day is interspersed with prayer, work, meals and recreation. There are five Franciscan charisms which we try to live by; the first is fraternity. Fraternity means we live as a family, as a brotherhood, and all the other things stem from this. The second is prayer and contemplation. Day and night, alone and in common we pray as brothers. The third is poverty and minority. We are friars minor; we try to seek the lowest place after the example of the 'Poverello', St Francis of Assisi. Again, when Padre Pio was asked who he was he often said, 'I'm just a poor friar who prays.' The fourth charism is ministry and apostolate; we are engaged in many different ministries at the service of the Jesus Christ and the Church and especially the poor. And the fifth charism is justice, peace and respect for the integrity of Creation. This was something that was very dear to the heart of Francis of Assisi. To love all the environment, plants, animals and humankind, as being created by God.

Today the life of a Capuchin friar is perhaps not as difficult as it was a long time ago. The daily life of the friars as I pointed out was taken up with prayer, Mass, work, recreation, and meals. On Fridays to this day, the friars renew their vows together in the refectory. In the past, there were also certain penances the friars practised in the choir and in the refectory on Fridays and days of penance. In the friary of San Giovanni Rotondo, Padre Pio would have participated in meditation and prayer in common, and in the common penances, and in the partaking of meals in common with the other friars. He would have shared in the housework, and in the refectory and around the house when his health permitted, and he would have been at the disposal of the guardian (superior) of the friary and of the provincial minister.

There was a time in his life in the mid-1930s when he was asked not to say Mass in public and hear confessions while these spiritual phenomena associated with him were being investigated by the order and by Church authorities. This was very hard on him, but he accepted it all as a penance and in obedience to the order and to the Church he loved. He was seldom alone in that over the day, he was with the friars at Mass, at prayer, at meals and at work and recreation. He had some friars who were close by to assist him and especially when his health was bad and when he suffered. All his life, he was regularly called upon to meet people for confessions and prayers.

I mentioned that the friars used to rise at midnight for the Midnight Office. Padre Pio was often awake during the early hours anticipating his early morning Mass which he offered before an increasing amount of people over the years. Eventually, because of the crowds, the friars had to build a bigger church, such were the numbers of pilgrims coming to his Mass. He heard men's confessions in the sacristy after his thanksgiving after Mass, and later in the morning he would hear women's confessions in the public church. As the years went on, people had to book a ticket to go to confession to Padre Pio. Here, he would enter the realm of the supernatural as he heard each confession. His compassion for those who were suffering because of a physical or a moral problem would come through. There were also moments when someone went to confession to Padre Pio for the wrong reasons or just out of curiosity. On these occasions he would have very little patience and would even refuse absolution, knowing that then was not the right time.

In the refectory, Padre Pio would join other friars for the midday meal. The dining room in the friary is set up differently in many places these days but in Padre Pio's time the superiors would sit at the top of the refectory and the other members of the community would sit at tables on each side of the refectory in order of seniority. Padre Pio was never guardian in the friary but was sometimes elected one of the house counsellors. The meal would begin by all the friars processing into the refectory and genuflecting and making the sign of the cross while the guardian would lead the grace before meals. On days of penance meals would be taken in silence and they would often be frugal and without meat. On these days of penance, like in Lent for example, a friar would read a passage of scripture, or a chapter from the life of St Francis of Assisi, or a part of the constitutions of the Capuchin Order. On other days and feast days, the friars would be allowed to talk and take a little wine with their meal.

One of our Irish Capuchin friars, the late Fr Peter Dempsey, studied during the war years in Rome. While all the students were unable to travel home that time, they were sent to different friaries in Italy. Fr Peter found himself in the friary of San Giovanni Rotondo. He often sat beside Padre Pio for the main meal and he regularly spoke to Padre Pio in Italian. Fr Peter told me that he found him very interesting to talk to and didn't get the impression of someone who had all these spiritual gifts from God. While he always wore the brown fingerless mittens, he came across as an ordinary friar among the community. Padre Pio told Fr Peter he prayed very much for the Church in Ireland and for the Irish Capuchin missionaries.

There's a short movie that has surfaced in the last few years, *Padre Pio – Rare Footage*, and it's available on YouTube. I believe it was filmed on cine camera in black and white and it's from around the middle of the 1950s. In it you can see what looks like an excellent account of a day in the life of the friars in San Giovanni Rotondo and how Padre Pio is simply a friar among them. There are also some scenes of people queueing to meet Padre Pio and also queueing to go to confession to him. There is a scene with Padre Pio saying Mass and at the altar. There are also scenes of him interacting with the other friars, even in humour and in good form as he swishes his cord as if to say with a quip, 'Get that camera away from me!' You can see him entering the refectory for the midday meal. When he comes in, he has to kneel down and kiss the floor before he takes his seat because he was late due to the volume of people wanting to see him. We then see the friars tucking into bowls of spaghetti and the wine bottles on the table in front of them.

Padre Pio was an ordinary friar who did extraordinary things. He seamlessly connected from our world to the next world in prayer and, while he suffered greatly, he offered it all up and believed that his sufferings were not a waste of time and could perhaps do some good. He spent many years helping to build the Home for the Relief of the Suffering, the great hospital in San Giovanni Rotondo which stands today as his legacy of care for those who suffer. All in all, he continued to live his life, day and night, as a 'poor friar who prays'.

Pentecost Sunday

THE BIRTHDAY OF THE CHURCH

In some ways, Pentecost Sunday, the birthday of the Church, a major Church occasion, is disadvantaged out there. We all understand Christmas Day more in terms of Christmas presents, Christmas cards, Christmas dinner, Christmas cake etc. We also get Easter too because of Easter eggs, the Easter Bunny and Easter parades.

In the lead into the Ascension, which we celebrated in the Church 10 days ago, we see Jesus reminding his disciples and followers that it is necessary for him to go. They were frightened and confused perhaps because they didn't want it all to end. They witnessed so many wonderful things that Jesus did in his public ministry; they literally saw people lifted out of paralysis, out of fear, out of poverty, out of death and out of sin. And now it was all over. Jesus reminded them that it was necessary that the Christ should suffer. This was something that they were afraid of too.

Before he ascended into heaven, he told them some things about the future.

From Matthew's Gospel we read 'Jesus said to his disciples, all authority in heaven and on earth has been given to me; go therefore and make disciples of all nations, baptising them in the name of the Father, and of the Son, and of the Holy Spirit, and teach them to observe all the commandments I have given to you. And know that I am with you always, yes, to the end of time ' (Matthew 28:19).

In the Gospel according to John, Jesus also said, 'I have told you all these things that you may find peace in me. In the world you will have trouble, but have courage, I have conquered the world ... ' (John 16:33).

Jesus had to go in order for the Holy Spirit to come down upon the Church. He said so again in John's Gospel: 'I tell you solemnly, it is for your benefit that I go because unless I go, the Advocate cannot come ... ' (John 16:7).

We believe that Pentecost is the birthday of the Church. While the disciples were for many days hidden in fear after the Resurrection of Jesus, they needed the power of the Holy Spirit to fortify them for this great mission. This power came upon them in the form of tongues of fire and it fuelled them for the mission ahead.

Our young people who are confirmed probably don't fully realise what this means, and, in fairness, while they learn about it in school and at home, I wonder if it sinks in beyond the nice clothes and the money. But it does work away there in the background. The seven gifts of the Holy Spirit work away in those confirmed each day of their lives.

In these days we are preparing for a constitutional referendum in Ireland. We are all encouraged to study all the facts and to be as informed as possible before we vote. On both sides of the debate; passionate and sincere people have highlighted honestly felt beliefs. For me, my belief is that the unborn child is made in God's image and likeness and has a right to life, so I am going to vote No.

We are all talking about the sermon Bishop Michael Curry preached at the royal wedding yesterday. He powerfully spoke of when love is the way. He said, 'We were made by a power of love.' He concluded his sermon by praying, 'And may God hold us all in those almighty hands of Love.'

Pentecost Sunday is the birthday of the Church and we all love to celebrate birthdays, they are important – especially to our younger people. We celebrate these special days because we have been born. We pray for the powerful love of the Holy Spirit to be with us all in these days and always. Amen.

Follow the Camino

I walk around most of the day. Like nearly all people, I've been walking since I learned to walk as a toddler. I have become better at walking in the last few years in a bid to lose weight and, by and large, it has paid dividends. To help in this regard, my family made me a present of a Fitbit to count my steps each day. The goal is 10,000. Yet the idea of walking the Camino of St James was somewhat intimidating in that it meant that I would have to walk from point A to point B and what would I encounter in between? While I know it's walking and not running, one has to be fit and relatively healthy because an average distance of 20 kilometres is covered each day and this can be in all weathers and over road, field and mountain track, as well as some climbs and descents. I first heard of the Camino de Santiago de Compostela in 1999, when two teachers I knew went out there at the start of their retirement. Rather than wake up in late August wondering about not returning to school for the first time in 40 years, they walked the way of St James into September and October.

Our decision to walk the Camino de Santiago de Compostela was my bright idea. Carmel Keogh, a parishioner, had walked the Camino in autumn 2016 and decided to raise money for the parish church restoration fund. While I was thanking her at Mass, I said maybe we should look at doing the Camino as a parish for the bicentenary in 2017? And there, it was out. Paddy Pender, our parish secretary, asked me later on if I was serious.

We began to look at what was involved, and we got in touch with Follow the Camino, who would help us to organise and plan the pilgrimage. From that far back, it never looks dangerous, and while the group came and did an information night with us, it still seemed so far down the road. Then time passed and we were walking together each Wednesday and Thursday, training and raising awareness of the 200th anniversary of the opening of the church and the Camino we were going to do. People began to come on board and express interest in doing the walk with us. It still seemed unreal because all of us have our own lives and commitments and the Camino was still 'out there'.

We would walk on Wednesdays from the Four Courts Luas stop along the tracks up to Infirmary Road, and return via Montpellier Hill and Arbour Hill or back along the tracks at Benburb Street and Smithfield. A nice walk which wasn't terribly challenging, but steadily we built up the miles over the winter and spring. Our team of walkers were me, Pauline, Paddy, Linda,and Carmel, not forgetting Jasper the dog. We didn't tell Jasper that he probably wouldn't be able to travel to Spain with us. All the while there were other enquiries and eventually the number committed to the Camino settled at 10. Follow the Camino made the necessary bookings for us in terms of transfers and hotels. I believe we did the sensible thing and made sure we had a place to rest and recover each evening.

The trip suddenly got very real for me when Paddy and I went over to Suffolk Street to the Follow the Camino office to pay the balance of the bill and then received our Camino kits. It hadn't fully sunk in for me, perhaps because I was distracted with so many other day-to-day things, but there was an excitement building at the same time. I tried to imagine what the walks would be like and the food along the way. I wondered would there be a place to say Mass for the group each evening and what the photo opportunities would be like along the routes. I was a total Camino newbie so I really only imagined what would be in store.

In preparation for the Mass on 25 August, we visited each area of the parish for house and family blessings. As we went around the areas on those fine summer evenings, we got to meet most of the neighbours and families. Many of the neighbours set up small altars and put out statues and holy pictures. And there was also hospitality and a cuppa at the end of the prayers. We were also reminded that some of the older parishioners who were housebound would like to see us and so it was a blessing to celebrate the Sacrament of the Sick with them. People were texting each other on the balconies of the flats to tell them that we were around, and I was called up to visit different homes and even to bless cars and pets!

We celebrated the Mass of thanksgiving on 25 August with invited clergy, friars, religious, parishioners and friends. It was a lovely occasion led by the Archbishop of Dublin, and we continued the celebrations in George's Hill with hospitality, chat and the cutting of a 200th-anniversary cake. Everyone was so kind and supportive along the way, especially during the painting and the decorating, and the ceremonies were a lovely backdrop to preparing to travel out to Spain to walk the Camino.

The final preparation days leading to our departure for Spain were spent getting advice and help from Dominic and Ruth from Army Bargains on Little Mary Street. This place has been there for years and Dominic couldn't have been more helpful in terms of boots, socks, leggings, T-shirts, rain gear, backpacks and walking poles. As we were being looked after by Follow the Camino we didn't need overnight camping gear, but Dominic was keeping an eye on all we needed for the long walks.

And so, 7 September arrived, and we all met in Dublin airport for a morning flight to Vigo on a Ryanair 737. We were delayed leaving

Dublin, but a good tailwind aloft meant that we made nice time en route down to Vigo. The approach into the small airport in Vigo is very mountainous and you could feel the drop every so often as we descended. In arrivals we were met by the representative of Follow the Camino and soon we were on the coach to the Hotel Colon in Tui, where we settled in and unpacked.

Most of us took a walk around the old town of Tui and got our pilgrim passports stamped in the stunning cathedral there, and Br Jeremy and I went to Mass that evening in the Dorothean Nuns' convent chapel. We freshened up and all met for our evening meal outside as the evening was fine and warm. Amazing how a one hour and forty-minute flight south can mean the difference between eating indoors and eating al fresco in September. It was an opportunity for us all to gather and meet since some of us hadn't met before. After a nice meal and a beer, we all headed in different directions for bed and made preparations to begin our walk in the morning. What to leave in the suitcase for transportation to the next hotel? What essentials to take in the backpack which might be needed for the journey along the way? And so off to sleep.

The next morning, Friday 8 September, the Feast of the Nativity of the Blessed Virgin Mary, we met for breakfast at 7.30 am and tried to eat well in preparation for a walk of around 20 kilometres. Jeremy set off an hour earlier, as he had threatened, and took some supplies with them to eat 'on the hoof'. After breakfast it was time to go and, after we had posed for a photo and posted it on our parish Facebook, we said a prayer to the Guardian Angels and Saint James and headed off on the first morning of our Camino adventure. I felt emotional as I began to walk up the street and towards the sunrise.

The streets were only waking up as we left the periphery of the town and as we walked the morning got brighter and brighter. It was a lovely feeling to be walking together and we all settled into a good pace as we headed out of Tui and made for O Porriño.

Along the way we made pit stops to drink water or eat something. Essentially, what we learned early on was to look out for stamps so we could mark our pilgrim passports. This is important to show the Pilgrim Office in Santiago de Compostela that we had passed by all these places along the Camino and really did walk all that way. In many cases stopping to rest is as important as eating and hydration is very necessary to keep up the energy. From the early kilometres on the walk we began to meet other pilgrims with the salutation 'Bon Camino!' We found ourselves sharing bread with Dutch, German, American, British, Australian, and fellow Irish pilgrims along the way. The last leg of the walk on the first day seemed endless as the route took us through an industrial estate and along a very long road. We were very relieved to arrive at the hotel in O Porriño and settle into our hotel rooms. They were very nice and gave us a room to have Mass together later in the evening. We freshened up and went out in the early afternoon for tapas before returning to the hotel to rest and for Mass and the evening meal.

The second morning we were pleasantly surprised to sit down to a fine breakfast and also doggie bags to take on our walk. For some, there was an added surprise as Barry's Tea was available for the Irish connoisseur away from home. We headed off on our second full day north out of O Porriño; this leg was going to take us 22 kilometres up to Arcade.

We again encountered many other walkers along the way and also when we stopped for a rest. Even when the language was a barrier, the Camino is a great meeting point; the fact that we were all walking, tired and sore meant we all had something in common. We met Grace from the Netherlands who told us she was attacked by a dog on the previous day and was bitten quite badly. The owner of the dog took her into the house and afterwards brought her to a hospital for the wound to be dressed. A dreadful experience for anyone at any time but no doubt compounded by walking the Camino.

We all chatted together and I began to hum the famous song 'Grace', based on the tragic relationship of 1916 Rising leader Joseph Mary Plunkett with Grace Gifford. I told the story and the group insisted I sing it for her which I did and, as we walked, we sang the song. She got me to sign my name on her backpack and since then she has blogged the meeting with the 'singing priest' and the Irish group! The next day we stopped in the woods where in a clearing there were two lads selling leather bracelets and Camino trinkets. One of them had a guitar and, as soon as he realised we were Irish, he gave us a fine rendition of 'The Wild Rover'. We also met a girl from Germany who walked with us for a while as we all shared our stories. Though we were only away for a week, it was still comfort food to meet other Irish pilgrims as we walked along and it was good to meet pilgrims from Blanchardstown and Ballinteer, as well as Roscommon and Cavan. The scallop shell of the Camino illustrates the myriad roads all going towards Santiago de Compostela, and it also shows how many different people one can meet along the way.

Leaving Arcade was one of the nicest parts of the walk as it was a beautiful morning and we all gathered before the old Roman bridge crossing over the wide river. I took out my camera to take some pictures. An old woman was selling Camino shells from the door of her house and I bought one as I passed along the way. Traditionally the scallop shell tells a story; it is used as a food utensil: a spoon, a soup bowl and something to cut food with. We climbed up through the old town along pretty streets and hanging baskets. All along the way we saw ripe grapes hanging on vines and some people harvesting them and we also saw large pumpkins growing in fields. People would say Galicia is like Ireland in its countryside but with the vines and pumpkins outdoors everywhere you go, you would soon realise that we are a little further south.

Given the time of the year and the location, the walks were manageable and while the days were fine, the sun wasn't too hot. We were glad to stop and rest in different places and have some water or iced tea and something to eat. We were surprised to find some places very busy with walkers and pilgrims and it was at times like this that we were glad to have travelled with a group like Follow the Camino where we knew that we had a place to stay each night. Meeting together in the evenings after a rest, to gather for Mass, and then for a meal was a blessing as we could give thanks for a good day. At Mass we held our parishioners in prayer as well as all who asked us to remember them along the way. It was also good to pray with other people we met as we walked. We had seen a group of women from the USA on our first night and over the days we encountered them on the roads and tracks. One morning we met them over breakfast in Pontevedra and they called me over to their table. One of the women must have heard I was a priest, so she asked me to pray with them as it was her birthday. So there and then, across the breakfast table we joined hands and prayed together. Obviously, the day was significant and poignant for her on the Camino away from home, but also because it was 11th September. We prayed for all who died as a result of the terrible attacks on New York, Washington,and Pennsylvania in 2001. We all realised that we were going on to Caldas de Reis that day and we arranged that they join us for Mass in the evening as we would be staying in the same hotel.

Sharing our stories as we walked along the way with the group we travelled with and also meeting others and walking with them was very special. There were moments which were charged with emotion; like the times we saw way points covered with prayer intentions written in different languages. At each way point, each of us would place a stone or a shell to either offer a prayer for some-one, or to let go of a painful memory and leave it behind. We also came across a place where someone had left behind walking shoes and a walking stick. One of our group said that this can often be a sign that a person just couldn't go on. This was less than 25 kilo-metres from Santiago de Compostela.

When we reached Santiago, tired, emotional and with sore feet, we made our way first to the cathedral where we were directed to the Pilgrimage Centre. We met a fussy attendant who was annoyed we were too late. With a bit of Irish coaxing, he agreed to process our passports and told us to come back later for collection. All I wanted was to get to the hotel and shower. Then, I looked forward to chang-ing into my habit and going to the cathedral for evening Mass.

As we left the pilgrim centre, we saw Grace, the woman from the Netherlands, in the distance walking towards us on the road. We all spotted her almost at the same time. Spontaneously, I started to sing the chorus of Joseph Mary Plunkett's 'Grace', which we had introduced to her some days before early on in our Camino. She looked around for the sound and when she saw us coming towards her, she dropped to her knees. Such was the emotion and the joyful tension, the relief and the tears at reaching our goal. We all hugged and chatted and wiped the tears from our eyes. We got to the hotel and freshened up and almost immediately headed for the cathedral for evening Mass.

I checked in at the office of the magnificent cathedral, showing my celebret to the sister at the entrance to this beautiful sacristy. Straight away, I met fellow priests; pilgrims all who had reached Santiago de Compostela in the days before. We chatted quietly until Mass time and signed our names in the sacristy register. While the Mass was in Spanish, I was asked to say part of the Eucharistic Prayer of the Mass in English. At the end of the Mass, I was moved by Robert, Anne and Carmel coming over to me, delighted to see me on the altar. They were saying how much of a privilege it was to be part of the group.

The following day, 14 September, the Feast of the Exaltation of Holy Cross, was our last day, and we came to the pilgrim Mass and again it was very powerful. This time the place was packed to capacity. People were standing along the aisles and all around the back and sides. At the end of the Mass, which again I concelebrated, they lit and swung the giant thurible to honour the feast day. This amused me as I had seen television footage from many years ago of the famous thurible being swung when Pope John Paul II had visited the cathedral. I was also amused when many of the priests concelebrating jumped to the front of the sanctuary to take photos and movies on their cell phones of the thurible going back and forth, swung by uniformed acolytes and assistants. Many of the pilgrims were doing the same from the body of the church, filming as the smoking thurible went left to right and right to left. Afterwards we went to pay a visit to the church of the Franciscan friars and spent some time there. Off then for a small bit of souvenir shopping.

And that was the end of the Camino. Leaving the cathedral and leaving the city I was genuinely sorry that it was all over. I'm a homebird. For me, the nicest journey is the journey home, and I can't put my finger on what it is, but this time it was like I was happy to be a pilgrim among other pilgrims. Many people can say categorically that if they didn't like a place, they would be reluctant to return. There are one or two places I wouldn't be that keen to return to. But the moment we landed back in Dublin, when asked would I do the Camino, I was saying; 'absolutely'. God willing some of us are going off again, this time to Viterbo in Italy to walk down to Rome.

THE BEATITUDES OF THE PILGRIM

Blessed are you, pilgrim, if you discover that the Camino opens your eyes to what is not seen.

Blessed are you, pilgrim, if what concerns you most is not to arrive, as to arrive with others.

Blessed are you, pilgrim, when you contemplate the 'Camino' and you discover it is full of names and dawns.

Blessed are you, pilgrim, because you have discovered that the authentic Camino begins when it is completed.

Blessed are you, pilgrim, if your knapsack is emptying of things and your heart does not know where to hang up so many feelings and emotions.

Blessed are you, pilgrim, if you discover that one step back to help another is more valuable than a hundred forward without seeing what is at your side.

Blessed are you, pilgrim, when you don't have words to give thanks for everything that surprises you at every twist and turn of the way.

Blessed are you, pilgrim, if you search for the truth and make of the Camino a life, and of your life a 'way', in search of the one who is the Way, the Truth, and the Life.

Blessed are you, pilgrim, if on the way you meet yourself and gift yourself with time, without rushing, so as not to disregard the image in your heart.

Blessed are you, pilgrim, if you discover that the Camino holds a lot of silence; and the silence of prayer; and the prayer of meeting with God who is waiting for you.

Pope Francis, Repair my Church

No doubt the historic but intensive apostolic visit of Pope Francis to the World Meeting of Families in 2018 in Ireland was a success. But a perusal of the media reporting and social media coverage since Pope Francis has returned to Rome highlights criticism by Archbishop Vigano as well as a sharp focus on how effective the Universal Church is in its management of child safeguarding.

While it is an imperative that the truth comes out on these important matters, specifically in relation to Archbishop Vigano, I cannot help but believe that the Holy Father is being subjected to a tactical attack by some in clerical leadership roles in the Church. I feel that they simply don't like him, and indeed have been critical of him since his first day as pope.

In the Gospel according to Matthew, at the Last Supper, Jesus turns to the disciples and prophesies that the 'Shepherd will be struck, and the sheep will be scattered' (Matthew 26:31).

In the second chapter of Matthew's Gospel, Herod learned of the birth of Jesus and wanted to kill him (Matthew 2:13). Almost from the beginning of his public ministry, the established faith leaders didn't like what Jesus stood for. They didn't like him eating with sinners, and they were critical of his association with lepers and tax collectors. They resented that he met people on the periphery and that he crossed borders to reach out to the poor. They watched for every opportunity to condemn him when he ministered on the sabbath. It made them angry when Jesus called them out for their hypocrisy. In a word, Jesus was brave.

When Jesus was condemned to death, Pilate didn't know him. The Romans in charge of the scourging and the execution didn't know him. The soldiers who drove the nails into his hands and feet didn't know him. The Pharisees and the scribes who were supposed know the Scriptures should have known him. Jesus' disciples who abandoned him certainly should have known him. At least they came back, and they repented because of the prayer of Christ. 'Simon, Simon, Satan has got his wish that he sift you all like wheat, but I have prayed for you, Simon, and after you have recovered, you in turn must strengthen your brothers' (Luke 22:31-32).

The very ones who are criticising Pope Francis are supposed to be shepherds; wouldn't you think they should know him? Instead of showing a leadership of service, it seems to me that some ministers in the Church would prefer to see the back of Pope Francis and this is very sad. There are some in ministry who feel Pope Francis is too liberal, dispensing with many of the exterior trappings of the papacy, living modestly, wearing a simpler cassock and sash, and wearing simpler vestments. Others feel he is still too conservative and should speak up in support of the prevailing culture of the world more, especially in the west.

While it is critical that the truth fully comes out, because the truth will set us free, it is very sad that some attack the Holy Father in public and chip away at his mission of service to the Church.

I get consolation from remembering the vast multitudes of 'God's holy and faithful people' (as Francis likes to call them) gathering at the faith, enriching Festival of Families in Croke Park last Saturday evening, and at the wonderful Papal Mass last Sunday. The people came to see the Holy Father from the four corners of the world – and our country – in the wind and rain, to hear in his words and see in his example, his desire to bring people closer to Jesus Christ. In the words of the Gospel for the Mass, 'Lord, to whom shall we go, you have the message of eternal life, and we have come to know that you are the Holy One of God' (John 6:68).

The vision of Pope Francis comes from the life of St Francis of Assisi when he kneels in prayer before the cross in the little ruined chapel of San Damiano. Francis hears the voice of Jesus which says 'Francis, go repair my Church which as you can see is falling completely into ruin.' At first, Francis begs for bricks and mortar to literally build up that ruined chapel. Later, with the help of the poor and marginalised, and with the help of the other brothers who came to join him, he discovers that Jesus means building up the Church, not with bricks and mortar, but person by person and by embracing the best parts.

Franciscans don't destroy, they repair. This is the vision of Pope Francis too, and his vision contains time, and care and prayer. Let us act on his request to us on that special day in August when he visited the Capuchin Day Centre in Dublin's city centre. Before giving his apostolic blessing to all present he said, 'Thank you for trusting us. Pray for the Capuchins, pray for priests, pray for bishops and pray for the Church.'

The Sorrowful Mysteries

When I was growing up, our family had a few addresses. I know this only too well these days when I have to complete another Garda vetting form. The number of places I've lived spills over the page and almost causes a time-out on the computer. I sometimes dislike being asked what part of Dublin I'm from, because growing up I lived in Santry, Kimmage, Kilnamanagh, Rialto and back to Kilnamanagh. But I, and my six siblings, Kevin, Gráinne, David, Aoife, Lorna and Clodagh, were all born between the canals in the Coombe Hospital. I was baptised in the Church of the Holy Child, Whitehall, by Fr Tom Stack. He later carried my baptismal candle in the offertory procession at my first Mass as a priest in 1997. I made my first Holy Communion in the school hall of St Kevin's school in Kilnamanagh in May 1977. The parish church hadn't been built yet. We moved to Rialto, and, in March 1982, I was confirmed by Archbishop Dermot Ryan in St James's Church.

My family were Sunday Mass-goers. We would have been known to the local clergy in each of the places we lived. Sometimes, if we didn't make the Mass in our local parish, we would all be put into the car and we would go to 12.45 pm in High Street, or 4 pm in Mount Argus. I vividly remember passing through town on Sunday evenings on the way to Granny Gretta's on Finglas Road. We used to go swimming in St Vincent's pool. My dad used to identify some of the churches along the way. One in particular would play a big part in my life later on, St Mary of the Angels, Church Street.

I remember on some Saturdays as a child going into Lourdes Grotto beside St Catherine's Church on Meath Street to pray. We would usually visit the grotto on the way back from Frawley's to Nana's house on O'Curry Road in the Tenters. Lourdes Grotto on Meath Street is a place that many Dubliners and Liberties people hold dear. Years later, when I preached at the Triduum in honour of the Mother of Good Counsel in John's Lane Church, I recalled being brought there, and to Lourdes Grotto, and seeing Pope John Paul II on Thomas Street in 1979 as he rode in the popemobile through the streets.

My Dad, Enda, would have volunteered in many of the parishes we lived in and the schools we went to, especially in Kimmage, Rialto and Kilnamanagh. I remember he used to do the sound for sports days and made reel-to-reel tapes to play music through the grey tubular speakers tied and suspended to poles. Dad used to make recordings on that old reel-to-reel tape deck. He kept the BASF tapes in a 'USA Assorted' biscuit tin. There were all sorts of things on them, including music and songs and us children talking and singing. He even kept the full live Johnny Cash gig he recorded as the sound man in the early 1960s from the National Stadium. Last year, my brother David sent an email to Tim Desmond from RTÉ's *The Doc on One* and, to cut a long story short, they took the tape, digitised it, and made a programme about Johnny Cash's lost concert which was then broadcast on RTÉ Radio early in the summer of 2018.

Lately, it has been haunting to hear again our voices as kids at one of the birthday parties in our house along with several of our friends as we did our party pieces. In an instant we were taken back in time to cartoons, songs and sayings from the late 1970s. It has also been great to hear the voices of some of my grandparents, now all gone to God. My dad taped them at some family gatherings before I was born. As I recall, one of his recordings was his parents' silver wedding anniversary in 1965. We hear my granddad (who died in 1977) giving a speech thanking all who came for their kind gifts. To laughter, he says he looks forward to celebrating their golden jubilee in 1990! We are all used to seeing old movies or hearing old songs from many years ago, but when you hear the voices of your relatives coming at you, especially from a time before video or internet, it is very special and, at the same time, quite sad.

When I joined the Capuchin Order in 1987, we used to say the Rosary in the evenings in the little friary church. Soon, like learning to drive and driving on our own for the first time, we were trusted to lead the prayers ourselves. Some of the lads weren't sure how to start the Rosary. As a former Legionary, I was not only able to say the Rosary, but I knew the different mysteries. However, I tended to begin the sorrowful mysteries automatically, because our junior group, or presidium, met in Benedicta House on the South Circular Road on Tuesday evenings and all Legion meetings begin with the Rosary. On Tuesdays we recited the sorrowful mysteries, so I guess it stuck to this day. I must say, of all the different mysteries: Joyful on Mondays and Saturdays, Sorrowful on Tuesdays and Fridays, Glorious on Wednesdays and Sundays, and Luminous on Thursdays, I still prefer the Sorrowful. I find them very easy to pray and imagine the scenes of Christ's passion.

Jesus Enjoys Being Generous

Jesus enjoys being generous and he seems to break the rules of general generosity. We see examples of generosity every day at home, at work, at school and in our day-to-day experience. We are also reminded of generosity in terms of the lack of it when we see meanness and self-centredness. From time to time we witness great acts of generosity when we hear of large donations being given to a charity or people paying something forward. I saw people in social media making conscious decisions to pay grocery bills for customers at check-out queues. We all have images of how someone's generosity can make another person or family happy.

If we look across the Gospels – the feeding of the five thousand (Matthew 14:13-21), the miraculous catch of fish (Luke 5) and the wedding feast of Cana (John 2:1-12) – we see Jesus displaying levels of extravagant generosity in paying attention to the needs of people. We see Jesus' generosity in how he is willing to forgive sinners, even where things get uncomfortable for him. He is unwilling to give the sinner a hard time or lay a guilt trip on him or her. Instead, he prefers to show people how to be happy going forward and sinning no more. Examples of Jesus' generous forgiveness and encouragement would be in the Good Samaritan (Luke 10:25-37), the return of the lost son (the Prodigal) (Luke 15:11-32) and the woman caught in adultery (John 8:1-11). In all these stories Jesus offers fresh insights into how God the Father loves us and asks us to love one another as a way of being happy. Jesus displays great generosity, too, in healing the sick and he even raises the dead, restoring them back to their families.

At the wedding at Cana in Galilee, Mary the Mother of Jesus realises there is a problem which would mean disaster to the hosts of the wedding. No different from today, weddings were important occasions in the life of the family, shared by relations and friends. To run out of anything, but especially wine, was unthinkable, yet this is precisely what happened in Cana. John tells us there were six stone water jars which were used for the ritual washing ahead of any meal and each had a capacity of 20 to 30 gallons. Jesus, after reminding his mother that his time had not yet come, tells the servants to fill the jars with water. They did this. Jesus tells them to draw some out and take it to the steward who tasted it and it had turned to wine.

A Google search of the amount of wine Jesus miraculously created tells us it was around 180 gallons, or 680 litres. This makes around 900 to 1,000 bottles, or 63 cases of wine, depending on the size of the bottle. And we know from John's Gospel that it was the 'best wine', so it wasn't cheap plonk, it was the best vintage.

Jesus seems to love being kind to people. He likes to be generous and likes to see us happy. He also reminds us that God the Father loves us and is interested in us and delights in us. It's as if Jesus rejoices in us, laughs when we laugh, is happy when we are happy, and strengthens us when we are sad. And Jesus urges us to follow his example with each other, and love one another, especially the ones who irritate us!

Over and Over Again

In Halston Street, when I stand at this ancient ambo to preach, I'm aware I have stood here many times since I became parish priest in 2010, and I am sure I have repeated myself quite a few times. I imagine some have said; 'Here we go again!'

I am reminded of the story told by Archbishop Fulton Sheen: a famous scientist was in great demand as a speaker and presenter. People would fill lecture rooms and auditoria just to hear what he had to say. He had a chauffeur who drove him to his sessions and indeed sat through all his presentations. He was invited to speak to a group of 400 scientists, and when he was being driven to the venue, the chauffeur said, 'I must have heard that presentation 1,000 times. I bet I could give that talk!' The scientist agreed and the two men swapped clothes and the chauffeur stood up and gave the presentation. He delivered a perfect, flawless talk and, at the end, was given a standing ovation. When the applause quietened the Q&A session started. One delegate stood up and asked a very complicated-sounding question: 'When you take that H_2SO_4 and mix it with the NACL and cross it with the photographic plates of the sun, how do you get the equation $E=mc^2$?' The chauffeur looked at him and said, 'That's the must stupid question I was ever asked, and to prove how stupid it is, I'm going to ask my chauffeur to answer it!'

When I get up to preach at Mass or whenever I'm invited to visit a parish, there is the hope that when I speak, I speak God's word, but I'm sure my ego gets in the way every now and then. At the moment, we're in Cycle C reading Luke's Gospel. Cycles A and B use the Gospels of Mark and Matthew. We use the Gospel of John a lot at Eastertime. Over the three cycles, we hear the same stories told in different ways. We get different views of the same events. There is a lot of repetition because Jesus wants to speak to our hearts and not our heads. As we hear the stories told and retold, they become part of us. As Pope Francis reminds us: 'Jesus desires to change the world one heart at a time.'

It is good to hear the word of God in a new way each time – the Gospel should hit us for six!

Today's Gospel is about the Final Judgement. When I was talking with my mother recently, she was saying that she grew up frightened at the threat of the fires of hell and everlasting damnation. Many of her contemporaries had that fear too. Catholic education and faith formation in Ireland in my parents' and grandparents' generation, while it had many good and positive aspects and attributes, it also had a negative part to play. The result is there are people crucified by scrupulosity for years and others fearful of the wrath of God. The truth is, we will be judged by how we have loved.

Jesus said to his disciples, 'When the Son of Man comes in his glory, escorted by all the angels, then he will take his seat on his throne of glory. All the nations will be assembled before him and he will separate men one from another as the shepherd separates sheep from goats. He will place the sheep on his right hand and the goats on his left.

'Then the King will say to those on his right hand, "Come, you whom my Father has blessed, take for your heritage the kingdom prepared for you since the foundation of the world. For I was hungry and you gave me food; I was thirsty and you gave me drink; I was a stranger and you made me welcome; naked and you clothed me, sick and you visited me, in prison and you came to see me." Then the virtuous will say to him in reply, "Lord, when did we see you hungry and feed you; or thirsty and give you drink? When did we see you a stranger and make you welcome; naked and clothe you; sick or in prison and go to see you?" And the King will answer, "I tell you solemnly, in so far as you did this to one of the least of these brothers of mine, you did it to me."

'Next he will say to those on his left hand, "Go away from me, with your curse upon you, to the eternal fire prepared for the devil and his angels. For I was hungry and you never gave me food; I was thirsty and you never gave me anything to drink; I was a stranger and you never made me welcome, naked and you never clothed me, sick and in prison and you never visited me." Then it will be their turn to ask, "Lord, when did we see you hungry or thirsty, a stranger or naked, sick or in prison, and did not come to your help?" Then he will answer, "I tell you solemnly, in so far as you neglected to do this to one of the least of these, you neglected to do it to me. And they will go away to eternal punishment, and the virtuous to eternal life."'(Matthew 25:31-46)

When we look at the Gospels, the stories come back to looking out for each other and the most surprising people become our teachers. The woman at the well was looked down upon, yet she became one of the greatest evangelists. From the moment she had her encounter with Jesus she spread the word about him throughout the area. We can love one another until the cows come home but it is hard to love those we don't like. Again, it's no harm to be reminded of God's love for us and how Jesus tells us this in the Gospels. There are many illustrations where Jesus paints an accurate picture of how much God loves us, and that God never closes the door to us. There are plenty of examples in the scriptures which come up often in the liturgical year where the 'sinner' who comes to Jesus for forgiveness and healing is often the one to proclaim the power of Jesus Christ to the people.

The Gospel story above is a principal way Mother Teresa and the Missionaries of Charity tried to work to look after the poorest of the poor. In these principles, she found a spiritual meaning to all that the sisters did. As well as the words of Jesus in Matthew 25, she also found great meaning in the peace prayer of Saint Francis of Assisi. The 'Anyway Poem' is also another prayer that was dear to Mother Teresa.

THE PEACE PRAYER OF ST FRANCIS

Lord, make me an instrument of your peace.
Where there is hatred, let me bring love.
Where there is offence, let me bring pardon.
Where there is discord, let me bring union.
Where there is error, let me bring truth.
Where there is doubt, let me bring faith.
Where there is despair, let me bring hope.
Where there is darkness, let me bring your light.
Where there is sadness, let me bring joy.
O Master, let me not seek as much
to be consoled as to console,
to be understood as to understand,
to be loved as to love,
for it is in giving that one receives,
it is in self-forgetting that one finds,
it is in pardoning that one is pardoned,
it is in dying that one is raised to eternal life.

THE ANYWAY POEM

People are often unreasonable, illogical and self-centred;
    Forgive them anyway.
If you are kind, people may accuse you of selfish, ulterior
    motives;
Be kind anyway.
If you are successful, you will win some false friends and
    some true enemies;
    Succeed anyway.
If you are honest and frank, people may cheat you;
    Be honest and frank anyway.
What you spend years building, someone could destroy
    overnight;
    Build anyway.
If you find serenity and happiness, they may be jealous;
    Be happy anyway.
The good you do today, people will often forget tomorrow;
    Do good anyway.
Give the world the best you have, and it may never be enough;
    Give the world the best you've got anyway.

You see, in the final analysis, it is between you and your God;
It was never between you and them anyway.

In his life on earth, Jesus applied the principles of charity to all
who came to him for healing and forgiveness. He went out of his
way to minister to all who were in need and he was extravagantly
generous in how he provided for people. It is reasonable, therefore,
based on the scriptures and the Gospel, that we will be judged by
this loving God based on charity. Yet, as we know, love can be painful. The pain and discomfort of love help us to grow and flourish.

There is a Latin phrase I think of here: *Recissa vegetor assurgit* – 'When we prune plants, they grow stronger'.

I remember when we were kids, we would be lined up at home to take Radiomulsion. I think it's gone off the market today in favour of all the soluble vitamins and ginseng etc. It was a yellow syrup with a bitter taste which contained multivitamins and all mammies gave it to their kids. We would stand in line, myself and my siblings, and Mam would fill a spoonful of the stuff as we waited our turn. We behaved like we were being force fed and made faces and jumped to the back of the queue. My brother even tried to escape to the garden in an explosion of histrionics. My mother reminded us that when she was a child, she and her sisters were lined up to take the castor oil. Nana consoled us by telling us tales of how the boys and girls used to eat their spinach with gusto because they would get strong like Popeye the Sailor. Many of my friends shared stories of having to take it growing up even though we hated it! The things that are good for us aren't always easy to take but we need them. The only question we need to worry about at the Final Judgement is 'Have you loved as in the Gospel?'

Jesus in the Desert

This weekend we have an interesting backdrop in our Gospel – the wilderness, the desert. Jesus spent a period of time in the desert before starting his public ministry: 'Jesus, full of the Holy Spirit, returned from the Jordan and was led by the Spirit in the wilderness, where for forty days he was tempted by the devil.'

To do something dangerous, something difficult, something that pushes us to the limit, we need to do our homework before embarking on it. To do a marathon we need to put in the hours of training, have proper nutrition and be hydrated. To climb a mountain, we need a different kind of training. Bear Grylls goes out into the wilderness and can make food and shelter out of what is available. When we head out to the wilderness, we need to know what we are doing. In the wilderness, we face our demons. Even though Jesus was fully God, he was also fully human, and the risks and dangers applied to him just as much as they would to you and me.

Jesus was led into the wilderness and there he was tempted by the devil. Despite all the promises the devil made, tempting and all as they sounded, Jesus knew they were not to be trusted. Jesus knew they were all lies because the devil is a liar.

In the first temptation, Jesus is tempted to eat bread and satisfy his earthly hunger. 'If you are the Son of God, command this stone to become a loaf of bread.' Jesus answered him, 'It is written, "One does not live by bread alone".' In time, contrast this with when we will frequently see Jesus sitting at table with people and providing food and drink in abundance for those who are in need. For now, however, despite his being tempted to eat, to satisfy his hunger, he will fast.

In the second temptation, Jesus is offered power, glory and a chance to be famous. Again, remember that Satan is a liar, and no one knows this better than Jesus. Even though Jesus is weak, tired and hungry, he is fuelled by the Spirit and he will again point away from himself to worship God the Father.

'To you I will give their glory and all this authority; for it has been given over to me, and I give it to anyone I please. If you, then, will worship me, it will all be yours.' Jesus answered him, 'It is written, 'Worship the Lord your God, and serve only him.'

People have always hero-worshipped movie stars and sports stars. Years ago, getting famous meant a lucky break in the film or music business and it could take a long time. Band managers visited loads of music shops buying records and filling the boot of their cars in order to get their charges higher and higher up the charts. Today, thanks to social media, people can find a faster way to the dizzy heights. An audition in the past came in record companies' studios or in the basement of a club. Today you can stand before Simon Cowell and Louis Walsh and a live TV audience and get catapulted quickly to a record deal and fame and fortune. As in the past, you still need luck. A Facebook page can lead to lots of 'Likes' and 'Friends', and the temptation is to get more and more 'Likes' and 'Friends'. It was nigh-on impossible to get your hero to notice you in the past. Today, on your smartphone, with a tweet, it is possible for movie stars, world leaders, politicians, sports stars and top bands to interact with you.

With Jesus, however, it is never about him. It is always about the Father. Jesus always points away from himself and points to the Father.

In the third temptation, Jesus is tempted to compromise his relationship with God.

'If you are the Son of God, throw yourself down from here, for it is written, "He will command his angels concerning you, to protect you," and "On their hands they will bear you up, so that you will not dash your foot against a stone". Jesus answered him, "It is said, 'Do not put the Lord your God to the test".'

Jesus won't buy into these temptations, but the three temptations are how the world operates and the world says, satisfy your hunger, seek fame and power. Jesus sees beauty on the inside, whether one wears designer clothes or clothes from the bargain basement. Jesus goes to the heart of who you are.

Going into the desert means taking time out and tuning in to what is in our soul. Going into the desert allows us to slow down and to plug in to the Spirit. Going into the desert, away from the noise, can help us to hear our heart again. The season of Lent is a going into the desert and there we stand close to Jesus who knows our struggles and our need for time out.

Come, Holy Spirit

We celebrated the Sacrament of Confirmation here in the parish recently and I have been reflecting on the power of this Sacrament. Our Capuchin provincial minister administered the Sacrament of Confirmation to the sixth-class pupils of the local school. I have no doubt that they were all sincere and happy to receive the Sacrament of Confirmation, but I am also sure that they didn't really know what was happening. I am confident they were well prepared; they have been working away since last autumn. They had the Ceremony of Light, they took the pledge, but I don't know if they really fully understood it all. As Church, we are beginning to have conversations about the future of the celebration of First Communion and Confirmation. I believe the time has come to celebrate these two important moments in our Christian lives within the family and the parish and not in school. Parents come to ask for their child to be baptised; dates are agreed, and the sacrament is celebrated in the midst of the parish. The same could happen with First Communion and Confirmation.

Few know what the Holy Spirit is really about. Fr Anthony de Mello told us that 'Every word, every image used for God is a distortion more than a description' (*One Minute Wisdom*). Since this is the case, it is even more difficult to understand the Holy Spirit. The Holy Spirit is the essence of God and that is BIG.

The children today received the Holy Spirit at their Baptisms, and they received the Holy Spirit again at their Confirmation. When we receive the Holy Spirit, it is something powerful and beautiful and we don't, I mean can't, see it. It's like Holiness hits us!

When I was thinking about the Holy Spirit, I began to think of Queen Elizabeth. There is a TV series on Netflix called *The Crown* and there is one scene when the queen is anointed at the moment of her coronation that is very powerful. The coronation of Queen Elizabeth at Westminster Abbey in 1953 was broadcast on television and people were very excited to have the chance to witness this very historic moment in their own homes. When it came to the time to anoint the young queen, a canopy was placed over her while the Archbishop of Canterbury anointed her. In the scene on Netflix, Edward, Duke of Windsor, the former King Edward VIII, is watching the live television images from Westminster Abbey from his home in France. The canopy is put over the queen as she is being anointed, the most sacred moment in the coronation ceremony. One of his guests asks why they don't get to see this and Edward says, 'Because we are mortals'.

The conferral of the Holy Spirit is so sacred, it is God entering us. Once a Sacrament is conferred, it cannot be undone. This is God's way of telling us that God will not let us down – I am with you always (Matthew 28). Our very essence changes when this happens. We become people of God. This is very, very BIG. We cannot merely learn about it. We need to pray for it too, pray to receive the gift of faith. When we pray, the Holy Spirit comes down on us.

The Spirit of God is a powerhouse. The Holy Spirit is the love between God the Father and God the Son; the Holy Spirit brings the love to life. The Holy Spirit is the power, the force, a creative power of pure love which you can't bridle. The Spirit of God was in this Church is a very powerful way as the Holy Spirit came down on the children. The provincial minister prayed over each of the children invoking the Holy Spirit: ' ... be sealed with the Gift of the Holy Spirit.'

The seven gifts of the Holy Spirit are with us since we were confirmed and support us as we go through life. We have wisdom and right judgement to help us make good choices; understanding for our relationships; wonder and awe in God's presence – awe of love of God in each of us; courage to be who we are meant to be; knowledge to know right from wrong; and piety – our powerhouse built on prayer.

For me, Pope Francis is a man of great courage, a man full of the Holy Spirit since he is not afraid. Saint Pope John Paul II was also a man of great courage and he too was full of the Holy Spirit. You might remember a story of the Christians who were taken captive by ISIS. Seven of the captives were paraded across a beach, wearing their orange jumpsuits and told to renounce God. Each of them in turn refused to renounce God, knowing that refusal would mean death. One of the seven captives wasn't in fact a Christian, and when his turn came, he told ISIS that he was an atheist but that he wanted to meet the God the other captives would not renounce, since this God must be something very special to have this power of love over his followers.

Sometimes people will say they cannot pray but we don't need to worry about this since the Spirit of God prays in us. It's not a problem especially when we are worried, tired, broken or whatever – the Spirit of God is constantly praying in us. 'The Spirit too helps us in our weakness, for we do not know how to pray properly, for the Spirit prays within us, groans that cannot be put into words ... ' (Romans 8:26-27).

> Come, Holy Spirit, from heaven shine forth with your
>   glorious light.
> Come, Father of the poor, come generous Spirit,
>   come light of our hearts.

Come from the four winds, O Spirit, come breath of God;
  disperse the shadows over us, renew and strengthen
  your people.
Father of the poor come to our poverty.
  Shower upon us the seven gifts of your grace.
  Be the light of our lives – oh come.
You are our only comforter, peace of the soul.
  In the heat you shade us; in our labour refresh us,
  and in trouble you are our strength.
Kindle in our hearts the flame of your love
  that in the darkness of the world it may glow and
  reach to all for ever. Amen.
  (*Berthier – Taizé*)

I Would Like to Talk about Death

I would like to talk to you about death. In the Gospel this evening, we are reassured that God has prepared a place for us in the Kingdom. But first a story from Archbishop Fulton Sheen:

A family man, an Irish American, was on his deathbed. All his life he was a quiet-spoken man, the strong and silent type. His sons were contacted and immediately started making their way home to be with him in his final hours. His sons were scattered throughout the USA, having completed their college education. Each son was as successful as the next and their father was very proud of them – given that he had a humble start in Roscommon before moving to Boston as a young man. One son was delayed due to the poor weather conditions. He spent a lonely evening all by himself in a hotel room and he rang one of his brothers from his hotel and heard the sad news.

'I'm sorry, but Dad just passed away'

'Oh, I so wanted to be there with you all, but the weather ... '

'I know, but you were with us in Spirit – we knew that.'

'Did Father have any last words? Anything?'

'No, there were no last words; Mother was with him to the end!'

The Kingdom of Heaven is very close to us and we ought to connect as best we can to those who have gone before us. Don't wait until we die to go to heaven but go there often by and through prayer.

Jesus is the way, the truth and the life. Jesus tells us so, but if going to heaven is so simple, so wonderful, so blissful – why are we afraid? It's because dying is one thing we have to do alone, yet our destiny is to be with God in heaven. Knowing there is a place for us in heaven helps us get through the weeks and days.

The Scripture readings we often use at funerals tell us of faith, generosity and quality of life. Death is a challenge. We won't see heaven with eyesight – in this moment, we only see with our eyes. We can see heaven with our hearts though – by insight. How? By loving each other and being there for each other. We have faith because someone loved us enough to pass on their faith to us. They didn't keep it for themselves – they passed it on. A seed is sown in us and the faith that is good enough for our parents and grandparents is good enough for me! So, we keep faith and we give it away ...

I speak to Jesus every day and I hear him in my heart. There is a place tailor-made for each of us in heaven, and our loved ones can see us from their new home in heaven.

When you were young, maybe messing in your room, being bold, your Mam and Dad always knew what you did even though they weren't in the room! You might go back into the kitchen and your mother straight away says, 'What were you up to? And before you say "nothing", I know what you were up to!' If parents can see with that kind of vision on earth, imagine the kind of powerful vision they have from heaven! And we'll pass that powerful faith on to others

Another short story; A woman in North London decided to get some work done in her house. She went away for a few days to let the workers get on with the job and when she got home, the foreman met her at the door. He asked her where she had gone, and she told him that she spent the few days on Iona, the Holy Island. 'Also known as The Thin Place', he said 'since the membrane between heaven and earth there is very thin.'

'Thin places' are places where we can go and connect. We can reach out to the love of God. Our ancient Irish ancestors knew of such places. When Christianity came to Ireland, the monks and sisters travelled to the lakes and mountains to connect to the world of God. Whether we visit a church, light a candle, open the scriptures, spend time before the Blessed Sacrament, take some quiet time, we have an opportunity to cross the small divide between earth and heaven. This is prayer.

Saint Joseph in the Ha'penny Place

Years ago, before I was ordained, a group of us went to Knock on pilgrimage. The group included some Young Franciscans from groups formed in many of the friaries in Ireland. The Young Franciscan Movement was very successful for a few years during the 1980s and 1990s and some went on to join the Secular Franciscan Order and other lay groups.

As part of the pilgrimage, many headed off to the Confession Chapel for Confession. Later on, people started to gather together and chat about their 'Knock experience'. The conversations turned to their experience of the confessional and one girl mentioned that at the end of her Confession, the priest said, 'And for your penance, I'd like you to say a prayer to St Joseph – no one prays to him any more!!' People pray to the likes of Padre Pio, St Thérèse, St Anthony and, of course, Our Lady. But poor St Joseph is often so far down the list.

But what do we know about St Joseph? Well, St Joseph is a man of few words. He is more a man of action – one who walks the walk rather than talking the talk. He has suffered so much during his life. He was betrothed to a beautiful girl and even though he discovered she was with child before they were married, he listened to God's voice speaking to him and believed God's promises for him and for his family. Joseph was probably the butt of the gossip machine in town, but he stood four-square behind Mary.

St Joseph has two feast days that are celebrated each year. On 19 March, we celebrate St Joseph, Husband of Mary, and on 1 May we celebrate St Joseph the Worker. We think of St Joseph working with his chisel, hammer and other tools of his trade, surrounded by sawdust with the boy Jesus by his side watching his every move. The boy Jesus would grow in prominence and take the front line while at the same time Joseph would withdraw from prominence.

The public image of the Holy Family is almost always an image of a wholesome, sterile group of people with a beautiful gaze in their eyes as they look at each other, but don't be fooled. St Luke's Gospel tells us some of the struggles they endured. It wasn't easy for the Holy Family. Some scholars have suggested that Joseph was an older man who died leaving a young widow and a son without a foster father.

Back to Knock! I was in Knock again recently and met two ladies that I knew. They had small statues of Sleeping St Joseph and gave me one. I didn't know, but Sleeping St Joseph is a favourite devotion of Pope Francis and he tells us:

> I would like to tell you something very personal, I have a great love for Saint Joseph because he is a man of silence and strength. On my table, I have the statue of Saint Joseph sleeping. Even when he is asleep, he is taking care of the church. Yes! We know that he can do that. So, when I have a problem, a difficulty, I write a little note and I put it underneath Saint Joseph so that he can dream about it. In other words, I tell him; pray for this problem.

Now I too write my prayer intentions on a piece of paper and place them under my statue of Sleeping St Joseph. Even when we are sleeping, God is at work on our behalf – for our own good.

ANOTHER CHANCE

There are some Gospel stories that I don't particularly get immediately. I much prefer when Jesus interacts with people and they come to him for healing and forgiveness. I also love how Jesus invites people to think again about the love of God the Father, particularly in the Parables. This weekend, the Third Sunday of Lent, Year C, we are invited to see how Jesus gives the fig tree one more chance (Luke 13:1-9). This fig tree is just taking up space and is not doing what it's supposed to do. People come to it for fruit and they find no fruit and go away disappointed. In the story, Jesus suggests leaving it another year, digging it round, manuring it and giving it a chance to bear fruit next year. At Mass, I suggested to the people that we need to look at the three readings together in their common theme in order to pick up on the overall message of Jesus in the liturgy.

In the first reading from Exodus (Exodus 3:1-8, 13-15), we see Moses tending the flocks of his father-in-law Jethro, a priest of Midian. After Moses had been banished from the court of Pharaoh, he found his way to the slopes of the holy mountain. These scenes give most of the content to the screenplay of Cecil B. De Mille's *The Ten Commandments*, starring Charlton Heston. While Moses is tending the flocks, the mountain begins to glow, and he climbs on to the slopes to see this phenomenon. He finds a bush there that is on fire but is not burning. Here he enters the presence of God. God utters the famous words, 'Moses, Moses! Take off your shoes, for the place on which you stand is Holy Ground.'

God gives Moses a mission to return to Egypt to tell Pharaoh to set the Hebrew people free. The people of Israel were in slavery in Egypt and God tells Moses that he has heard their cry to be free of their slave-drivers. In a sense, God has chosen Moses to be his instrument and he will free Israel from bondage in Egypt. God reveals his name to Moses 'I Am who I Am.'

The second reading picks some themes from the Liturgy of the Word and looks a little deeper at them. In the first letter to the Corinthians (1 Corinthians 10:1–6, 10–12), Paul reminds them of the story of salvation in the book of Exodus, that God provides a saviour who will deliver his people from their bondage. However, this bondage, this slavery, is also a slavery in sin. When we are caught in sin, it traps us and prevents us from being fully alive. We find it difficult to move and we can't fill our lungs with the fresh air of the Holy Spirit. We need a saviour from outside to come to our help. When we cut our finger, we need a plaster from outside. When we get sick, we need medicine from the outside to help our bodies to heal. And when we are hurt in a spiritual or psychological way, we need counselling or therapy from the outside to help us to heal and get better.

Time and time again in the Scriptures the people of God sin and fall short of the covenant that was agreed. God still calls the people back and the people repent and begin again. Our human nature makes us do wrong and uncharitable things, so we need help with God's grace. Once and for all God sends a Saviour to his people to save them from their sins. Jesus Christ is the Saviour who restores us to right-relationship with God again.

In the Gospel, taking into account the first reading and the second reading, and the responsorial psalm (Psalm 102:1–4, 6–8,11) – the Lord is compassion and love – we can be confident that when Jesus tells the people a parable, he speaks of the true image of God the Father.

Luke reminds us that the mission of Jesus recalls that the people are in constant need of a saviour. Jesus always gives us the benefit of the doubt and he calls his followers to keep their hearts open to the needs of the sinner. Pope Francis has picked up on this regularly in the six years since he was elected pope, and not least in his calling an Extraordinary Jubilee Year of Mercy 2015–16. Like the farmer who hears the frustrations of those who go to the fig tree and, finding no figs, call for it to be cut down, Jesus says give it another chance. With a little minding and ministry, who knows what good we can all do?

Plane Spotting

My first memory of seeing an aeroplane was in the back garden of our house in Santry Close when I must have been no more than two years old. I can still see it, a white and green Aer Lingus jet plane. It was on approach to the old runway 23 at Dublin Airport and I can still clearly see it in my memory. Because we lived so close to the airport, we got to go to watch the aircraft landing and taking off. In the 1970s when I was a small boy, the noise was powerful, and the smell of kerosene is something that still brings me right back to the excitement I felt sitting along the back road, as we called it. From that vantage point, I got to know the difference between the aircraft types, the airlines and the places they may have been going to. This interest has lived in me since then and I still love planes. People like me would be known as plane spotters or AvGeeks.

When I was about 12, I got an airband radio receiver for Christmas and my uncle Paddy, who was an engineer at Dublin Air Traffic Control, tuned in the radio frequencies for me: Dublin Central, Dublin Approach and Dublin Ground. What a thrill it was to hear the conversations between the controllers in the tower and the pilots. When I got older, I used to get two buses on some Saturdays to the airport with my radio, my binoculars and my little notebook for taking the registration of the planes I spotted. On those days, my school bag would become my plane bag, complete with Tayto crisps, sandwiches and a bottle of Coke. Once the spring came, I was off to Dublin Airport when the evenings got brighter, and when I got to the terminal building, or round the back to the runway, I would be busy spotting. I still have the bigger notebook that I transferred all the registrations into. With the Civil Aircraft Markings book I checked off the planes I had seen. I loved the Aer Lingus BAC 1-11s. I still remember their registrations: EI-ANE, EI-ANF, EI-ANG, and EI-ANH. Like all Aer Lingus planes, they were named after Irish saints, so these were named *Mel*, *Malachy*, *Declan* and *Ronan*. I also spotted the Aer Lingus Boeing 737s. They had the -200 series that time and, like the 1-11s, they made a lot of noise.

Most of the planes coming into Dublin when I was a boy were from the UK and Europe and were therefore more-or-less short haul aircraft. Aer Lingus, British Airways, British Midland, Air France, KLM, Lufthansa, Alitalia and Iberia would all be regular visitors.

When a big jet came in, there was great excitement. We often saw the Aer Lingus Jumbos. *Patrick*, *Brigid* and *Colmcille*. *Patrick* was the one Pope John Paul II arrived on in 1979. They dwarfed the other aircraft and, to this day, the Boeing 747 is my favourite plane. It is still known as the 'Queen of the Skies'. I remember spotting some of the bigger jets on Saturdays back then. Delta used to fly in from Atlanta regularly with Lockheed Tri-Stars, and Northwest Orient came in from Minneapolis-Saint Paul with Boeing 747s. There was an Iberia 747, too, in on a holiday charter which was always great to see since their long-haul jets would never fly to Dublin.

Parked over in the corner roughly where Terminal 2 is located now, Aer Turas kept their stretch Douglas DC8. It was a long four engine machine and it took cargo and freight to far-flung places. I remember seeing it take off a lot and it made a great sound on the tax-iways and on the take-off roll. Before the noise reduction of modern engine technology and before the emissions laws, these planes gave off a high-pitched whistle and a trail of black smoke as they lifted off into the sky, and on a clear day you could see the trail for miles.

I got to fly on an Aer Lingus Boeing 747 from Dublin to Shannon in 1984 – my first time on a plane. We flew at 16,000 feet at 400 miles per hour and got down to Shannon in 20 minutes. A small hop but it was something I will never forget. One of the cabin crew asked the captain could I visit the flight deck before take-off. I briefly got to experience a world I had never seen before; the cockpit of a 747-100 Jumbo with the captain sitting on the right, the first officer on the left, and the flight engineer behind the first officer. I was spellbound. However, there was no time for pleasantries as the flight crew were preparing to go but, equally excited, I took my seat in the cabin. I had no idea what the feeling would be like on the take-off roll and the experience of being pushed back into the seat thrilled me. As the plane gained speed, the nose was raised, and we began the climb out. I didn't have a window seat on my first flight so as soon as I was allowed, I spent the very brief cruise in a vacant seat by a window and took it all in down to Shannon. In those days, Aer Lingus landed at Shannon to collect passengers before the plane took off again for the transatlantic leg.

Unless you lived near Heathrow or Charles de Gaulle, Paris, or Kennedy in New York, you would never see the famous Concorde. In its flying history, it only visited Dublin three or four times. I got to see it in September 1995 when it made a pit stop with the winning European Ryder Cup team. I think it was an Air France Concorde. I remember seeing it on approach to Heathrow when I was working in London in 1993. I usually look up if I see a plane, but this took me by surprise when I looked up. It was a pity we didn't have smartphones at the time. I have visited Heathrow a few times over the years and, since they retired the Concorde in October 2003, it is possible to see one of them, G-BOAB, parked near Runway 27L. I find it sad that the Concorde is retired, especially following the tragic crash in

Paris in July 2000, and while I never got to fly on it, I hope to visit one of them some day.

We are into spring again these days in Ireland and I look forward to going on my weekly visit alongside the main runway at Dublin airport. I take my bag as I did all those years ago but this time there is a camera and the smartphone. I have seen some fantastic sunsets sitting watching the landing aircraft coming in from the west on Runway 10 when the weather is fine or there is an easterly wind. Add to that a jet on finals with the setting sun in the background. It is my happy place. There are exciting things happening for Dublin Airport. In the last few years, the new Terminal 2 is up and running and most of the 'heavies,' the large jets, are parked there. The Dublin Airport Authority has built the new tower at 86.9 metres high. They have turned the sod on the northerly runway which will mean being able to cope with higher volumes of landing traffic as well as parallel traffic taking off at the same time. For an 'AvGeek' like me, it means more planes to spot and more activity on the airfield to photograph.

I was never chaplain to the Defence Forces, but I've heard somewhere the 'padre' is known as a 'skypilot'. An interesting name, especially for a priest who is mad about planes and flying. While I have taken flying lessons, I am quite content to sit alongside the runway and watch the jets take off and land and maybe get a nice picture to share on the aviation social media pages. The noise of the engines, even though they are much quieter now, then in the past. The smell of kerosene still reminds me of why I love being up at the airport and why I still remember the lines and the beauty of an aeroplane that I loved as a boy.

Wear this Ring

MOTHER'S DAY

It must be very difficult to be pope today. He is up there alongside the queen of England and the president of the USA in terms of world fame. I would argue that this was probably always the case, but it has to be more intense in today's world since the advent of social media. The American president tweets daily to his almost 60 million followers and, in most cases, it provokes widespread reaction. The pope also tweets in different languages, although not personally, to around 47 million. The world watches famous people very closely and all they need to do is make a mistake and smartphones have the ability to share the unflattering picture or video. At the same time, Twitter, for example, has afforded many famous names the ability to set the record straight when a tabloid breaks a story the celebrity feels is untrue.

Pope Francis speaks and the world hears what he says. He is often misunderstood and, while the sound bite can make the headlines, the entire piece can get short-circuited. It was no different for Benedict XVI and indeed John Paul II. Certainly, the internet grew up during the pontificate of John Paul II. His homilies, speeches, and addresses, as well as his papal documents, are readily available for download on the Holy See's website. Thanks to the web, we have access to thousands of photos of popes with the faithful from all over the world. Today, it is popular for people who want to get the elusive selfie with Pope Francis if they manage to get close to him. I imagine that he himself would prefer no selfies if he had his way.

Recently, footage appeared that was shared on social media of Pope Francis receiving people who wanted to kiss the papal ring. It quickly made the mainstream media and news media. Some channels showed edited parts of the footage and not the whole piece. In it we see the pope taking his right hand away from people as they lean down to kiss the papal ring. A far cry from the days when people would approach the papal throne and drop to the ground and kiss the pope's foot. Francis is far more eager to lean down and kiss the feet of the sinner, and people who are broken of all faiths and none. This isn't something he does for the cameras either. He has done this in the past in his time as Archbishop of Buenos Aires.

Since Pope John XXIII, we have seen more user-friendly papacies in terms of how human and approachable the pope is. Pope John would chat to the gardeners and the workers in the Vatican. On the day he was elected pope in 1958 (for which he wrote an entry in his diary) when he was dressing in the papal white, he removed his cardinal's scarlet skullcap and placed it on a monsignor (thus making him a cardinal!). When John died in 1962, Cardinal Giovanni Battista Montini, Archbishop of Milan, became pope, taking the name Paul VI, and began to dismantle the trappings of the papacy. He wore a more simple, modern 'triple tiara' at his inauguration and eventually preferred not to be carried around aloft in the Sedia Gestatoria. In August 1978, when Paul VI died, Cardinal Albino Luciani, Archbishop of Venice, was elected pope and took the name John Paul. Although he was only pope for 33 days, he refused to wear any triple tiara crown. Cardinal Karol Wojtyla was elected pope on 16 October 1978 and took the name John Paul II. He was driven around in the now famous popemobile. He wasn't interested in people kneeling to kiss the papal ring and neither was Benedict XVI in his time (2005–13).

Going back to the papal ring, when Pope St Pius X (1835–1914) was ordained Bishop of Mantua in 1884, he went to see his mother, Margarita, at the family home in Riese where he grew up. As the neighbours called in to the little house to see the new bishop, they knelt to kiss the episcopal ring. His mother is said to have remarked,as she showed the wedding ring on her left hand, that he wouldn't be wearing any bishop's ring had she not first had her wedding ring.

I seem to recall hearing about the ceremony for the episcopal ordination of Angelo De Donatis as auxiliary bishop of the diocese of Rome in the Lateran Basilica in 2015. Before the pope put the ring on the finger of the new bishop and said the prayer, Francis quietly said to him, 'Don't forget the wedding rings of your parents and defend the family.' Pope Francis has got the right idea in that he sees himself in a ministry of service and leads by example time and again. Any trappings of ministry must remind us, especially as we draw closer to Easter, that Jesus Christ came not to be served, but to serve, and to give his life as a ransom for many (Matthew 20:28).

The wedding rings of our parents, the symbols of commitment mean that from day one, they were our first teachers and that they taught us by example. Any one of rank, pope, cardinal, king, queen, president, prime minister etc., had a mother and a father or was brought up by a parent or guardian or a family who came from a family themselves.

Finally, returning to Margarita Sanson, the mother of Pope St Pius X, and how she reminded her son of her role in his vocation by showing him her wedding ring. Happy Mother's Day to all mothers and grandmothers and remembering all mothers in heaven.

We Do Death Well in Ireland

We do death well here. As Irish people, as Dubliners, and as people of this parish. We do death well. Paddy, our parish secretary, tells me I've said this before. It's true, I'm like a broken record. And for those of you that don't know what a record is, or what a broken record sounds like, Google it!

But we do death well. And when we come to funeral Masses, you all turn up and you all sit in the same places. This is because the one who has died is one of your own. You may not be blood relatives, but you are family in a sense.

Jesus died a horrible death. I used to think modern generations didn't know much about the barbarity of Roman crucifixion. However, we see violence all too often in our society now, and we hear of senseless and evil murders like what is played out close to our communities and like Lyra McKee's death in Derry the other night.

But Jesus' death wasn't in vain. All through the Gospel, Jesus reminded the disciples that the Christ would have to suffer. He called them to faith in him. Death would not be the end. In the Gospel he calls Martha to faith when he says, 'I am the resurrection and the life' (John 11:25). He tells Thomas;, 'I am the way, the truth and the life' (John 14:5).

Those who witnessed the crucifixion were horrified and traumatised. All the disciples went into hiding. They played the awful scenes over and over in their minds. They talked about it and were confused, they thought it was the end. Until the third day.

Early on Sunday morning, the women who were going to anoint the body saw the stone had been rolled back. They went in and they saw that Jesus wasn't there. They saw a vision of angels who told then that Jesus is risen. They rushed away to tell the disciples.

Peter and John rushed to the tomb and found it empty. They all began to come to faith in the risen Christ. Dark tombs and old walls can't contain the risen Jesus. The tomb is open, the disciples see the place where Jesus was laid and they remember that Jesus said that the Christ would have to suffer, to be crucified, but on the third day rise again.

Every day I witness your simple but powerful faith here in the parish, especially at times of death and bereavement. Most of the time your doors are open. You all have a ministry of welcome and hospitality. Like the stone, which was rolled away from the tomb, the doors to your homes are open and you welcome people in. But you also go out to reach out to the friends and neighbours.

This is the way we fight back against the evil and violence we witness in our society and our world. We do it with love and light. We crowd it out by expelling it from the darkness of the tomb out into the light of Christ in the world. We spread the love. Thanks to all of you who spread that love on social media. It is truly good news. This is how Jesus is alive in our families, our parish, our city, our country and our world.

Lyra's partner Sara Canning spoke of her legacy living on in the light she's left behind.

The many Parisians singing the Hail Mary as Notre Dame burned was another example of the light of the resurrection.

And we give thanks to our parents who passed on the light of faith to us. Faith that Jesus Christ is the resurrection and the life.

Going Back in Time

After Jesus rose from the dead, different people encountered him along the way. Whether it was at the empty tomb, or when the disciples were gathered together in the upper room, or along the road to Emmaus. The Gospel for last Sunday (Third Sunday of Easter, Year C) from John 21:1–18, tells us of another encounter of the risen Jesus, but this time it is by the Sea of Tiberias. A few of the disciples of Jesus are together and Peter decides he's going fishing. The others said they would go with him. They went fishing just like they did before they met Jesus. Jesus himself stands on the lakeshore but they don't recognise him.

When I was small, my dad brought myself and my brother, Kevin, to see *Star Wars* in the Classic Cinema up from Harold's Cross when it was released in 1977. I still remember we queued up to get in to the 'pictures' as we called it. In 1985, as teenagers, we queued up for another movie, *Back to the Future*. This was a story about a Californian high-school student, Marty McFly, who loved his rock music and his guitar and his girlfriend, Jennifer. His friend, eccentric scientist Doctor Emmet Brown invents a time machine made out of a De Lorean motorcar and, with the aid of a 'Flux Capacitor', a device powered by plutonium which is inserted into the car, they are able to travel in time back to 1955.

Where would you go if you were able to travel through time? Would you go to meet one of the major figures of world history? Maybe attend the scenes of history being made? Would you perhaps go and be around for the first gigs of your favourite recording artists? Or would you go back to straighten out a quarrel with someone which has lasted to this day? Since we are imagining it is possible to travel through time, then we can go forward and see future winning horses in Cheltenham and Aintree and even see the winning lottery numbers!

However, it is not possible to travel through time like that. For one, the future doesn't exist and the only place we all live in is the now. But we can go back in time and, through different experiences, it is possible to be instantly taken back to childhood memories or places we've been.

I was over with the family the other evening and one of my sisters was up with her two children. The younger one, a baby boy, is four months old. My mother was trying to get him to sleep after a feed and she was walking him up and down as she sang to him. All the while she was saying, 'Sshhh … ' as the little guy settled. The conversation in the house quietened down. It took me back 40 years to when my younger siblings (one of whom is now the mother of these two) came along and there we were playing quietly while the baby was getting to sleep. The sound of the television was down low, the fire was lighting, the dinner was cooking, and there was steam on the kitchen windows.

I can't imagine going back to a time in my life and not having met the people I know and love now. How could we manage now if we had not developed the skills or learned all we have over the years? A musician would miss out on having learned the rudiments of the skill they now know and love.

The disciples gathered on the shore of the Sea of Tiberias that day were lost and confused. By going fishing it was as if they were going back in time to a place before they knew Jesus. Was it as if they never knew him? Then Jesus himself stands on the seashore and calls out to them. Even after the years they spent with him, the things they all experienced, and the times they had together, they didn't recognise him. They need to be reminded. So he asks them if they have caught anything? The answer is 'No.' He invites them to throw their nets out to starboard. Straight away, they net a huge catch. The penny drops. Immediately John, the beloved disciple, recognises Jesus. Peter reacts quickly and soon they all begin to remember what it is like being with Jesus. It is Jesus himself, the one who died and rose again at Easter, who reminds us of the difference he makes when we walk with him on our journey through life.

Panick Attack[3]

This was written as an attempt to lay out my feelings following a panic attack I had while saying Mass in May 2005. I remember it was a very frightening thing. I've spoken to others who have had panic attacks, and all agree that they are very scary. For anyone, and especially for those who suffer from them regularly, they cause huge anxiety and there are websites and social media pages dedicated to those who suffer. There is also help for those so that they don't suffer in silence. In my case, it happened during Mass, in the period between the Gospel and the offertory of the Mass and I honestly thought I was going to collapse and die. In those seconds, I saw myself being stretchered out and onto an ambulance, to the nearest emergency department. All these emotions happen in a period of about three to four minutes, but when we are in the middle of the panic attack, it feels like it will never end and if it does end, it will end badly. As you will see, no one seemed to notice anything about me. The maelstrom happening was happening inside me and it sucked a huge amount of energy and enthusiasm from me for a period of time.

In the following days and weeks, I felt vulnerable, tired, emotional and embarrassed. I also felt that 'they' (whoever they were) would now see that I didn't have what it takes to be guardian of a friary, or a member of the Provincial Council anymore. I was also worried that these were the signs that I wanted to leave the order.

---

3   Written in 2005

Most worrying of all, though, was that the enthusiasm I had for pastoral ministry (saying Mass, preaching etc.) was gone and I had no interest in these things. I didn't want to be feeling like that and was angry that some of the most important things in my life could be removed from me.

As the summer went on, and as I began to rest and recover, I gradually found my energies again. Receiving spiritual direction and pastoral supervision was and continues to be a big help in recharging the batteries. I remember at the start of the summer, when I was in the height of it, saying that I hoped I never go back to that friary again. I even shared it with some of the friars and they just listened and I'm grateful to them. I'm looking back at all this with the benefit of hindsight writing these words 14 years later. Did I ever get another panic attack? Yes, I did, but not as badly. Of course, I'm 14 years older and I've done some other things since then. I've been in hospital chaplaincy, done another stint as guardian of a friary, and another stint on the provincial council, and, to date, parish ministry. Humanly speaking, I get a reminder sometimes of my vulnerabilities. I just take a deep breath and try to see it pass. I sometimes take my relic of St Padre Pio with me onto the altar. I keep my relic of St Pius X in my rosary beads pouch, which gives me strength. Thinking about some of the greatest saints and pastors and how they sometimes struggled helps greatly too. We are not alone, and we all get scared sometimes.

MISTER NICE GUY

I guess I could have seen it coming. I certainly felt it although I wasn't sure if it would hit. It did and when that happened, I had no idea just what way it would hit.

To begin at the beginning would be impossible so I feel that I should begin some time before it hit, if you like. I am someone who finds it hard to say no. Another way of putting it is I try to be 'mister nice guy' and a bit of a people pleaser. I will take on things because it's quicker and easier to say yes and, let's face it, I feel that people will like me for saying yes. Afterwards I will feel angry with myself for saying yes to something that might be inconvenient for me.

TAKING ON TOO MUCH

An example of this would be agreeing to help out by taking on a Mass and confessions on Mondays in Cork city centre although I have already at least one Mass in our friary and two classes in the school. On the first Monday of every month, there is also the deanery meeting with all the priests, usually from 11 am to 1 pm and, coupled with that, there is the supply Mass. In the evenings of the first Monday of the month there is the Secular Franciscan Order, the meeting of the men and women of the Third Order of St Francis, which may or may not include a Mass. So, it is clear that Mondays and first Mondays of the month are busy anyway without the extra load of the supply.

Another example would be that on some Saturday evenings I have taken on extra Masses. At the beginning of my time in Cork (2001–7), I was approached by the neo-catechumenate community. They asked me would I be interested in helping them by celebrating their Eucharist on Saturday nights. I agreed, and I must say I found the experience at times different and refreshing. They plan and organise the whole liturgy and all I have to do is say the Mass part. The trouble is that I may have had at least one Mass already on Saturday. They are in two or three different communities (at different levels on their faith-journey in 'The Way', as they call their neo-catechumenate life), so their catechists need two or three priests each Saturday night for Masses for each group.

I have, on several occasions, also supplied for a hospital chaplain in Cork city and that has meant a 7.15 pm Mass there. Frequently, I would rush from there to the neo-catechumenate Mass afterwards. This also may be after the 6 pm evening Mass in the friary and again, it might be after the 10 am Mass that morning too. I have found myself sneaking back into the friary on a few occasions after these 'unofficial' supplies. I know best, yet here I am sneaking in, tired, cranky and hoping to get into the room to leave down the alb and take off the habit.

I used to be more afraid to go to the doctor about things, although I never really needed to go to the doctor before. I had chest infection/flu in early 2001 and since I went to Cork in autumn 2001 I have been to the doctors for the flu jab each year. In mid-2003, I had the blood pressure taken and it was reading high. I had suspected high blood pressure and, on further investigation, with a 24 -our monitor it was found to be normal overall. My cholesterol was high too, but I didn't need medication to get it down, I began to walk and exercise. I still struggle to do this although I am now back in Weight Watchers.

THE PANIC ATTACKS

I had what I feel was my first panic attack the night I arrived at Kilkenny as a novice in the order in September 1988. I can remember feeling scared and my heart began to beat faster. I thought I was going to die, and I remember thinking, 'I'll go home tomorrow'. When the morning came along, I didn't go home, and I eventually settled in. One warm night in Italy on a pilgrimage in summer 2000, I had a kind of panic attack, manifested as light-headedness, jelly legs, the floor sloping quickly under me, rapid heartbeat and shortness of breath. I had one again on a couple of occasions in bed late at night in the friary in the last six months. I had one in Mahon Point shopping centre when the family were down at the end of April 2005.

The one that frightened me most happened on the altar on Saturday 7 May 2005 during the 10 am Mass. I was coming to the end of the Gospel reading and I noticed it beginning with small butterflies in my stomach, and as I crossed over to the altar to begin the offertory it seemed to get much worse. I had all the symptoms I described earlier although I thought it was something physical. I thought I was going to collapse and thought I was going to die. I was wondering could any of the people notice it. As the attack went on, I continued to say the Mass and I noticed that the people seemed to be oblivious to it. One of the friars who was concelebrating the Mass didn't seem to notice a thing. I clearly remember in the midst of my drama twice thinking I'd need to ask someone to help me and perhaps some of the reasons why I didn't was that I was afraid and embarrassed, and I couldn't think what exactly to tell the people. And another reason was that I was beginning to say to myself that 'this is a panic attack' and 'this will pass'. This all seemed to happen over the course of two to three minutes, although I thought it would never stop and that the end of Mass couldn't come quick enough! As I proceeded through the Mass and into the Consecration, with no reduction in the prayers to God not to let me die, I noticed that my breathing seemed to be returning to normal and I was panicking less and less.

I remember wondering did another friar in the community who was sitting in the congregation notice anything strange about me. I was calming down right enough, and I was acknowledging that yes, perhaps this was not a physical problem, maybe, but a panic attack altogether.

By the time Mass was over I went back to my room and sat alone with my thoughts and fears, running the whole thing over and over in my mind. I was replaying the symptoms, poring over what had happened, checking out the fact that I was up for meditation earlier and there was no sign of my feeling that bad until after the Mass started. I asked the friar did he notice anything strange about me at Mass and he said no. I told him about the panic attack and, to be honest, he did make some comment about what I said but I can't recall what it was. I was tempted to call the GP but I was afraid he'd ask to see me and spot something physical. Then I tried to reassure myself that it was 'only' a panic attack and 'Sure that's all, why would I bother the doctor with that'? Anyway, I remember phoning one of my best friends in the order and telling him the story and he told me it was my body talking and to 'get out'. I made the usual excuses: 'I will during the holidays'; 'After the exams start'; 'I'm needed for the prize-giving ceremony in the School'. All the excuses I could muster up I threw at him. He told me to phone another friend in the order who knows me well, and that he would check back with me to see if I did phone. Of course, I laughed to myself and knew I'd be reluctant to do this. I phoned home and told Mam the story and she reassured me that this was natural and that I should try to come away for a break. I felt better after that phone call.

I then had the evening Mass looming and the two Sunday Masses in the morning. How would I cope there? Would I get another panic attack? My stress levels were fairly high I'd say because I was afraid, and I was giving out to God, asking why this had to happen to me. I can learn to cope with panic attacks, but why did it have to happen on the altar at Mass where there's nowhere to run? The nature of a lot of my work is public, so why did this have to rear its ugly head? The friar did phone back and immediately made the offer of a priest-friar from his community who would be available to slot in for me, but I told him that I would not go just yet.

THE DAYS AFTER

After the Masses and dinner on Sunday, which I barely touched, I went to Gurranabraher, a parish on the north side of Cork city which the friars run, for the golden jubilee celebrations of the parish. It was a big occasion and it was a concelebration which I took part in. I was in bits and a little emotional, totally tired and worn out. I remember two things clearly about that day. I was frightened because I had no interest in being there, I didn't feel part of the thing at all and, in fact, I felt scared and shaky. I also remember noticing the parish priest giving his introduction and standing to the forefront of the crowd. Normally I would love to be in the thick of the action. On that day I was glad to be hiding and wishing it was over. I remember thinking I would feel terrified if I was in the spotlight. After the Mass, I went straight back to the friary, preferring to avoid the festivities and the 'garden party' atmosphere.

The next morning, I phoned a friar friend to tell him the story and he encouraged me to take some time off. I told him I was very tired and that I really needed to get away. I phoned home and told Mam that I would be home on Tuesday. I got a text message from all the family wishing me well and this was a great support to me. I remember feeling emotional and weepy when I read the text messages. I went over to the principal of the school here and had a word with him about the whole situation and told him I really had to get out and take a break. I told him that I would miss the graduation and prize-giving night and that I would ask one of the friars who is chairperson of the board of management of the school, and another friar assisting as chaplain in the school with me, to look after the end-of-year Mass. I really couldn't see myself staying on, either in the house or the school, once I made the decision to get away. I phoned another local friar who is guardian of our main Cork friary in the city centre and told him the story on the phone and asked him to get someone to look after the Masses. I also asked him to do a baptism I had agreed to do on the following Sunday. He felt that it was a good idea for me to go away and told me not to worry about the Mass the next morning, that he would come and say it.

THE BEGINNING OF THE BREAK

I drove to Dublin and I can remember wondering how it would be when I arrived. I felt a little sick in the stomach and a bit apprehensive about how the immediate future was going to go. At that point, I was not sure how long I was going to take. I knew that I'd have to be back in Cork for the Provincial Council meeting on 18 and 19 May. I put those dates out of my mind and concentrated on getting some kind of headspace at home and in a different environment.

When I arrived home, I felt a little emotional but there was great excitement from them all really. There was a great welcome back and, to be fair, I was relieved to be home and to have come this far. I told them all what had happened over the previous two days and it felt like I was going over and over it like the rewinding and replaying of a tape. This didn't stress me at all but what I did find was that I was so zapped that I was finding it hard to recount all the details.

As the days started to go along, I was talking to some of the family about how I was feeling, and I was trying to get a handle on just how I was feeling. It was hard to understand what was going on in me but one thing that was standing out was that I didn't want to go back to the friary for a while. I can also remember the family asking was this symptomatic of some kind of vocations crisis. I remember I felt scared and almost horrified that they would ask this. Yet, alone with my thoughts, I began thinking of what it might be like to leave but at the same time knowing at the back of it all that I loved being a Capuchin.

COMING DOWN TO EARTH BY DEGREES

There's no doubt about it but staying with family can bring you down to earth fast. While I was welcome, and while they were a great support to me and my troubles, I soon learned that they are all struggling too. They struggle with their relationships, with careers, with mortgages and with finance. I haven't the monopoly on struggle, and I do acknowledge that in many ways I have it so much easier. I know this up to a point, but I need to be reminded from time to time.

On the evening I arrived, I received a call on the mobile from one of the friars in Church Street inviting me to meet him for lunch the next day. While I was glad that he was reaching out, I was fearful of explaining how I felt as it so was hard to describe.

The next day I met my friend and we went for lunch in the Smithfield Village. When we sat down, I, as typical as ever when I'm nervous, couldn't really eat, although I managed okay. I remember telling him how I felt although I was conscious that I needed to be honest. My friend knows me very well and he was totally supportive. He told me that when we were on the phone, he was eager that I take a week off and relax, but now, having seen me, he said I looked completely 'bunched' and he felt that I should take a complete break for the whole summer. He suggested thinking about doing what I'd enjoy and encouraged me not to think of returning to the friary and to rest completely. I told him I had taken on the St Anthony Novena in St Francis Church in Cork at the beginning of June. He told me that he would get someone else to do this. I was now officially off and on an extended break and that was that. He suggested having a word with the provincial minister and telling him about what had happened and saying to him that I needed to take an extended rest over the summer. He said that this would be supported, and the friary would be catered for.

When I got home, I told them what had happened and while I was satisfied with the meeting, and I felt I had said my piece, deep down I was still uneasy. I remember my mother and my brother Kevin asking me if there was still something the matter. The question of my vocation came up again and I told them that deep down I felt I didn't want to leave. Their point was that if I was heard and supported, then why wasn't I happier at least? In hindsight, I believe I still felt bad then because it was only three days after the whole emotional thing happened. It was still too soon to be able to make decisions and to see things clearly. I was looking forward to some kind of a holiday and at the same time I wasn't. I didn't want to be vulnerable. I feared the thought of returning to the friary, and I was afraid of visiting friaries. At that point, I was scared of saying public Mass or preaching and I had no energy for pastoral ministry or priestly work. But all the while I was craving normality. I wanted this awful time to be over. I wished it had never happened. Why did it have to happen? I hated being me in this situation. I didn't know this Bryan Shortall, and I didn't want to get to know him.

RUNWAY 10/28, DUBLIN AIRPORT

Life meandered along and I settled into a long break. I went over to the airport and spotted planes a lot of the days. Just looking back at my logbook, I frequently visited the airport and parked in my usual spot along Dublin's main active runway, 10/28. There I turned on my air band radios and had my binoculars at the ready for the logging of any commercial aircraft markings. I usually stopped in the Statoil in Ballymun and picked up some kind of lunch. Crisps and a newspaper were also an essential part of the pastime. It was then that I'd be ready for a few hours spotting planes and the possibilities of seeing previously unseen aircraft landing and taking off. Sitting by the runway and spotting planes taking off and landing is one of the things I enjoy most, and it's something that helps me to relax and chill out.

While I was parked alongside the runway, I remember thinking about the future months and feeling quite scared of the unknown. The 'what-ifs' came into my mind. What if I can't settle down in Cork again? What if I can't settle back into the order again? What if panic attacks on the altar don't allow me to say Mass or preach any more? I became conscious of some weddings and baptisms, and among them the birth and baptism of my niece Louise. What if I can't cope with these events and get scared or want to run away? These were scary thoughts, and when I was alone in the car at the airport on those May days, I felt tormented by these feelings.

I also visited Mount Argus, the Passionist church in Kimmage where we were brought as small children. I have a great love for that church and I always feel comfortable in the peace and quiet there. I spent some hours over the summer there writing and praying about how I felt at the time. In those journals, I wrote down how I was feeling and tried to see what the Lord was saying to me in the midst of all my emotion, confusion and fear. Again, I hated feeling the way I felt. I wished that this wasn't happening. One of the memories that I have as I sat and tried to pray in Mount Argus one evening is seeing the brother sacristan coming out and setting the altar for Mass. He was placing the missal on the altar and lighting the candles and I began to wonder what it would be like if I had to say Mass for a church full of people. As I relaxed, I felt comfortable with the thought of saying Mass in public there. I can describe the feeling as warm and right, and this helped me a lot. On those days of quiet prayer in Mount Argus, close to the tomb of St Charles, I allowed myself to feel I was getting stronger once again. Some negative thoughts still came into my head, like having to stand before a big crowd on a Sunday Mass, but thinking of how many priests and others do it day-in and day-out only made me even more determined.

THE PROVINCIAL COUNCIL MEETING

The provincial council assists the provincial minister in his ministry to the friars of the province. The members are elected at the provincial chapter. I was a member of the provincial council for the first time from 2004 to 2007. The time came for the May council meeting and I drove down with another member of the council. I was nervous of going to the meeting but at the same time I was not over stressed about it. We got to Cork before mid-day, and I was invited to stay in our friary in Cork city centre. After lunch, I drove down to the friary, arriving at the end of dinner, and I went into the dining room where the lads were finishing up. They all said hello, and asked me how the break was going, and how I was doing. After checking a few things and going through the mail etc., I headed back for the meeting. Back in Trinity, we began the council meeting in the usual format with a 'check in'. This gives us all a chance to say how we feel coming into the meeting. Naturally, I had a few things to say and, in fairness to the other members, they were all supportive and sympathetic.

BACK TO REALITY AND NEW LIFE

At this point it was 19 May and we celebrated my father's birthday, and the next day, 20 May, my niece Louise Mary was born. This was a great joy for the whole family and she was a beautiful baby.

A TRIP TO BELFAST

I had arranged to go for a few days to Belfast to see the friars there and so, a day or two after Louise was born, I cleared off for the best part of a week. We have a friary in a new and modified house in Lagmore Estate, Dunmurry, in Belfast. I was still at sixes and sevens within myself and the friars there knew this and were sympathetic, yet they weren't handling me with kid gloves. While I was there, one of my friends, the guardian of the friary, was honouring some commitments to say Masses for Franciscan sisters who were on a kind of intercultural peace course. I remember going with him to the Masses and I was conscious of feeling nervous during them. He said both Masses on the two days and I sat with the sisters and quietly concelebrated. Although I was glad not to be the main celebrant, I remember wishing that I was more up for it and less fearful.

PART OF MY POVERTY AND THE CROSS

The next morning, the news was coming through of a horrific crash involving a school bus in County Meath. Several young girls were killed on their way to school and I remember feeling desperately sad and emotional over the whole situation. Again, it really put my troubles into perspective, and I remember admonishing myself to cop on. I also remember asking the classic question: 'Why did God allow this terrible tragedy to happen to these young people, in the prime of their lives, many about to sit their Leaving Certificate exams?' This scared me because it begged other questions, about the tsunami that killed over 100,000 just after Christmas 2004, and the earthquake in Pakistan which also killed so many. It's hard to make sense of a loving, personal God in all this, and why would he be bothered with my problems, which are minuscule in comparison with so many people who are truly heartbroken?

We went out for the day to the Giant's Causeway and the Carrick-a-Rede rope bridge. It was a beautiful early summer's day and to see the stunning beauty of that part of Northern Ireland was fabulous. It was also very interesting to note that there, we were only 12 miles from the coast of Scotland and the Mull of Kintyre was clearly visible across the water. I chatted about my experience over the previous few weeks and wondered out loud why this should happen to me. I told my friend that over the previous weeks all sorts of thoughts came up. I said that I'm not afraid to consider any possibilities, but deep down I'm not really interested in any other life outside the order. I said I just don't want to be afraid of preaching or saying Mass. I don't want to get a panic attack again on the altar or at any function I do as a priest. Sitting on the Giant's Causeway,

I remember him saying that maybe that's a cross the Lord wants me to carry. Maybe I have to learn to accept it as part of the vow of poverty, and not pray for it to be taken from me. I must say I felt better coming away from the Giant's Causeway that day. Acceptance builds up inner strength.

The next few days were spent exploring Belfast and learning what a lovely city it actually is, with the Peace Process getting stronger day by day. I took a Belfast Tour Bus which brought us around the Docklands and the old Harland and Wolff shipyards where they told us plans are in motion for a major Titanic museum. From there we saw the Waterfront Hall and the Odyssey Arena. The Lagan is dammed upstream and the level of the water stays high which makes it a beautiful feature. We then took in the areas where the Troubles had left such a devastating mark; the Protestant Shankill Road, the peace lines and the Catholic Falls Road. The tour ended via Queens University and 'Holy Lands',' the student quarter. This sounds more like an advertisement for the Northern Ireland Tourist Board, but as I look back over last summer, I can see these were the times when I began 'coming into land' after so much confusion.

KILKENNY

I returned from Belfast and the weeks sped by as I made trips to Kilkenny where I stayed for a week, and to Carlow, where I spent a couple of days. When I go to Carlow, I always make a visit to the Poor Clare nuns in the town. They are always good to the friars, not just in Carlow but to all of us. They have prayed for me and supported me all the way through my time in the order. I don't know what I'd do without the assistance of their prayers and I know many people would agree. In Kilkenny, I met one of the friars in the community who I look up to and respect. We were together in Priorswood Parish close to Dublin Airport before I was moved to Blanchardstown in 1999. This man is quite simply one of the finest friars I know and a great priest. A big man with a heart of gold, he's someone I would go to in any crisis and I was delighted to meet up with him. One of the trips we made while I was there was to see an elderly friar who was ill in hospital in Thomastown. Thomastown and Inistioge in Kilkenny are perhaps two of the most beautiful parts of the world. We went in to see this man, a gentleman and a popular priest, and one of the oldest members of the Irish Capuchin Province, who had had a stroke and was very confused. We chatted for a while and he was confused between the past and the present. Sadly, he died a little over a month later. Before I left to return to Dublin, we went for a drive to Graiguenamanagh in County Kilkenny to see Duiske Abbey, one of the oldest Cistercian foundations in Ireland, and now a parish church. We took in Inistioge on the way back to the friary.

'BOW YOUR HEAD WHEN YOU SAY RIALTO'

Essential on the itinerary whenever I visit Kilkenny is to go to Foulkstown cemetery to visit the Capuchin plot there. I go to visit the grave of Fr Senan Dooley and say a prayer to him. Like Br Seraphin, RIP, another holy friar who was from Cavan who is buried there, I believe Senan is a saint and I'm not the only one who feels this way. Senan was loved and respected by many people the length and breadth of the country. We once travelled with him in the car from Cork back to Dublin. We must have stopped to call in to friends of Senan in nearly every second town on the way, so much so that it took us nine hours to drive back!

Senan was guardian of Church Street when we were student friars there. He was a real Dubliner with a great sense of humour and someone who was a great pastoral priest-friar. He was not very old when he died suddenly back in December 2000 in the Mater Hospital in Dublin, when we all thought he was getting better. I missed his funeral because I was giving a day retreat to the Secular Franciscan Order members in Maynooth the day he was buried from Kilkenny Friary, where he was guardian at the time. Senan was from Rialto Cottages, in Dublin's south city centre and he was very proud of being from there. He used to say with a belly-laugh, 'Bow your head when you say Rialto.' Some time ago, I took some clay from the banks of the old Grand Canal extension, where the Luas Red Line is under construction, and I spread it out over his grave, just so he might feel at home under a 'little bit of Dublin' This is probably a bit sentimental, yes, but I think it was a nice idea. I ask him to pray for me and us all now, as I do whenever I drop by Foulkstown.

One of the things I was advised to do over the summer was to pare back on the different commitments I had made over the years in Rochestown. Was there anything I was doing that I didn't need to continue? During my break in Kilkenny, I wrote a few letters to different groups telling them that I wouldn't be able to help them out for Mass again come September. I don't mind admitting that I felt I was letting people down or disappointing them but overall, I was glad to have made the decision.

On 16 July, we baptised baby Louise in Kilnamanagh, Dublin, and I was delighted about this for a few reasons. It was a special occasion for all our family and Kevin, Tracey and her older brother, Sam. I did my first public liturgy since the panic attack and I was feeling a lot more confident. It was also important to try not to wallow in my woes and to forget about myself, which I feel I succeeded in doing. We had a great extended family gathering back at Kevin and Tracey's place afterwards and Kevin had the house and garden looking very well. He had hoped that the weather would be favourable and of course it was.

THE CAPUCHIN REUNION

The feast of the Capuchin saint, Laurence of Brindisi, is on 21 July, and traditionally on or near that day each year we have a reunion of all the friars in one of our friaries. It's a chance for many of our missionaries who are in Ireland on holidays to get together and after a concelebrated Mass, there is a celebratory meal. As many of our missionary friars are home only every two to three years from Zambia, South Africa, New Zealand, Korea and California, some would not see each other for many years. Some years ago, at a missionary reunion in Church Street, two friars who were in formation together hadn't met in over 20 years as one went to Zambia, and the other went to California. They had each been home on leave over the years, but they were never at home during the same time. In 2005, the reunion was in Rochestown. I travelled back to Cork a few days beforehand and I admit that I was anxious about that. Was I ready to go back? Would I settle in? Would I like being back? All these different thoughts were going through my head and I was hoping to settle in and get on with it. I decided that after the reunion I would come away again for a couple of weeks and then return to Cork before travelling to World Youth Day in mid-August.

The reunion day was a lovely affair. The friary community had been coordinating the hospitality. One of the members has a great gift for making the friars welcome and was renowned for it. He had the place looking very well and, along with our friary staff, we all rowed in to get things organised. I prepared the liturgy with our organist who played the music for the Mass. The provincial minister was the chief celebrant and we had over 25 friars there from Ireland and overseas. Weather-wise, it was a beautiful day and friars were enjoying pre-dinner refreshments out in the garden and there was great banter and craic from young and old alike. I was delighted at how the whole day went and many of the friars came to me on the day and afterwards and congratulated me for a lovely day. It was a combined effort, but I was thrilled because it meant a lot to me and I wanted to show the friars that I was okay, and more than okay.

The friar who preached gave a very powerful homily on the vulnerabilities we all have as human beings. It was something that came from his heart and, listening to it, I'd swear he was talking about me and my story, especially my recent story. He told me that friars came up to him after the Mass on 21 July and thanked him and some even wondered was he talking about them. In truth, he was telling his own story and, further, he was telling the story of anyone who could call themselves a human being, with the struggles and the fears that every person has.

I stayed around Cork for the next couple of weeks where I had a wedding at Gouganebarra, the picturesque shrine of St Finbarr in County Cork. I travelled to Dublin on 5 August where I made remote preparations to go to Cologne for World Youth Day. I had another wedding in Kildare and yet another baptism in Kilnamanagh, so I was really trying to get back into it. Weddings and baptisms for friends are liturgies that I really enjoy because I get a chance to catch up with old friends and I feel privileged to be part of their special day.

WORLD YOUTH DAY 2005 – FROM DUBLIN TO COLOGNE VIA BELGIUM

From 14 to 22 August, I travelled, along with three young people, to Cologne to celebrate World Youth Day (WYD). World Youth Day was established by Pope John Paul II in 1984 as a way for the pope to gather with young people and to speak to them personally. Since 1984 International WYD has criss-crossed the world to places like Rome, Rio de Janeiro, Czestochowa, Denver, Manila and Toronto.

Our provincial minister suggested we sponsor three young people to travel with me. So, myself, two sisters from Cork and our vocations contact, who was preparing to join the order in September, linked up with the Catholic Youth Care in Dublin and travelled on eight buses from Arran Quay early on Sunday morning via Dun Laoghaire and Holyhead across the UK to Dover, arriving there at 1 am on Monday. We sailed to Calais in France and crossed to Belgium where we stopped off at Maredsous, the Benedictine monastery where Dubliner Blessed Columba Marmion was abbot until his death in 1923. There we had Mass for the Feast of the Assumption with the abbot and monks of Maredsous at 11 am, in which the chief celebrant was Cardinal Desmond Connell, Archbishop Emeritus of Dublin, who preached in English and French.

We arrived in Cologne in the evening and we gathered in the Parish of St Nicholas where most of the Irish and Polish pilgrims were based. Archbishop Diarmuid Martin of Dublin was chief celebrant at a Mass at 8 pm in the parish church in which he welcomed the young people on their pilgrimage in Cologne, in German and English, and recalled the contribution of Pope John Paul II to WYD. And pilgrimage was the operative word! I spent my first night in Cologne on the floor of a local gymnasium school along with 30 other lads. When you're used to en suite facilities as I have been for the last four years, the poverty of sharing one toilet and handbasin and no shower really stings, especially after nearly 30 hours on a coach.

CAFÉ CAPPUCCINO AND GERMAN HOSPITALITY

The next morning, I set out to find my main reason for being there. Early in the New Year, some German friars contacted the Provincial Minister with an idea to set up a Capuchin presence at WYD. The idea of setting up 'Café Cappuccino', named thanks to Blessed Marco of Aviano OFM Cap., would be a place where we could be seen as living the Gospel of Jesus Christ among the many young people there.

Blessed Marco of Aviano OFM Cap., beatified on 27 April 2003, rallied Catholics and Protestants on the eve of the Battle of Vienna in 1683, which was crucial in halting the advance of Turkish soldiers into Europe. Following the victory, the Viennese reportedly found sacks of coffee abandoned by the enemy, and finding it too strong for their taste, diluted it with cream and honey. The brown drink reminded the Viennese of the habit of the Capuchins, and the Viennese named it cappuccino in honour of the order.

Anyway, the German friars organising it were asking for volunteers to come and staff the café. So, on 16 August, I found myself in the shadow of the mighty cathedral of Cologne, where tradition has it that the relics of the three Magi are housed in a beautifully ornate reliquary. The café was just over to the right of the majestic cathedral, across the cathedral square and although the square was thronged with groups of singing young people, complete with their national flags, I had no trouble finding it as there were 'high visibility' friars both outside and inside the café. There was a fantastic Franciscan welcome for me, and I was quickly shown the ropes by Brothers Harald, Jeremias and Andreas, who were the coordinators of the enterprise.

I was soon serving creamy coffees, iced tea, mineral water, and Tau-shaped biscuits (courtesy of the Capuchin Poor Clares, who were dispensed from their enclosure for the week to come among the young people and facilitate prayer and meditation in a local parish church). There were also more than 20,000 vocations leaflets to be given out to all who called in and passed by the doors of the café. We worked in teams of eight or nine friars at a time, and those who weren't working the café shift were ministering over at the local parish church of St Kunibert, offering the Sacrament of Confession in different languages. During the week I met up with friars who worked in the café, and visitors from many provinces, including

France, Germany, Poland, Italy, UK, Australia,and the USA. For that week the café itself was open from 8 am until 2 am the following morning, Tuesday until Friday. The evenings at the café usually ended with music and a singsong in different languages on the pavement outside, while many young people passed by and joined in. I was glad of the hospitality of a host family, again arranged by the German friars, where we were really welcomed and made feel at home. And talk about hospitality; the Family Sauerwald went above and beyond the call of duty to make the friars feel at home. They moved out of their home and into their camper van in order to give over their home and their beds to us. Over the week I called over to the Irish group to say hello and to join in on some of the liturgies and the catechesis there. On the days I joined with the Irish group the catechesis was given by Archbishop Diarmuid Martin, Bishop Jim Moriarty of Kildare and Leighlin and Cardinal Roger Mahony of Los Angeles.

'THANK YOU, J.P. 2'

There were so many highlights for me during the week, it would impossible to list them all, but I will mention two; the three-storey high banner of Pope John Paul II which hung across the square in front of the Cathedral, simply saying 'Thank you, J.P. 2'. It hung on one side of an office block, while another banner with the new pope, Benedict, saying 'welcome', hung on the other . The other obvious highlight was of course the final liturgies of WYD at a place called Marienfeld, about 20 kilometres outside Cologne. The new pope, Benedict XVI, arrived in Germany late in the week of WYD and was taken up the River Rhine in a barge as we stood on the banks cheering him on. Two of the Irish pilgrims were asked to be part of the international group in the barge with the pope. Later, I saw him driving through the streets of Cologne in the famous popemobile.

MARIENFELD – THE FIELD OF MARY

I travelled over to join with the Irish group on the Saturday morning as the café was closed and we went in our convoy of coaches, complete with tricolours flying. The group leaders told us that we would not be able to get right into the pilgrimage field with the coaches but that they would take us as far as possible, and hopefully we wouldn't have to walk too far. We alighted from our coaches and walked for four hours to get there, so finally it felt like a pilgrimage! We (and what looked like the rest of the world) arrived in Marienfeld at about 5 pm, totally exhausted, and we were promised a good view up at the front, near the altar. God bless the Italians; you need to be up early to get in before them and, needless to say, they were there first and they were not for moving. Plan B was not so good, but we did the best we could and ended up at the back about a kilometre and a half from the altar. We set up the Irish tricolour on a large stick so that we could use it as a landmark should any of us get lost. As far as the eye could see, there were people with sleeping bags and tents. I've never seen anything like the crowds since Pope John Paul II came to the Phoenix Park in 1979, although I was just 10 years old then.

POPE BENEDICT XVI ARRIVES!

At last the sun started to go down and the choirs were singing from the altar area and thankfully there were lots of big screens to see all the action. There was a real sense of celebration and praise as the choirs sang in many different languages. The cameras began to switch their focus from the choir to a white high-roofed van coming into the altar area, and the cheers and roars began. Pope Benedict XVI had arrived!

I have to admit, the hairs stood up on the back of my neck and I was reminded in my emotion and excitement of other 'hair on the back of the neck' moments, sacred and secular, in my recent years. Standing and cheering in the old common room in Church Street, celebrating with the brothers, some now gone to God, the evening Ireland beat Romania to get into the quarter-finals of the World Cup at Italia '90. The night we all watched Riverdance, the interval act in the 1994 Eurovision Song Contest, which became more of a talking point then the winning act. And being in Rome for the beatification and canonisation of St Pio with Frs Brian Browne and Albert Hayes of happy memory.

The new pope celebrated a vigil in the presence of the Blessed Sacrament, and he urged the young people to focus on Christ and his Real Presence. He said that in the Sacred Host 'Jesus becomes the bread that sustains and feeds us.' Pope Benedict then celebrated Benediction of the Blessed Sacrament and sang it in beautiful sonorous Latin which held many of the young people spellbound. Being present that evening at Vespers and Benediction with Pope Benedict in Marienfeld, I knew again that I was meant to be there with the Irish pilgrims and being part of the Capuchin project for WYD. When all is said and done, I was glad I was a Capuchin friar because I would be lost being anywhere else doing anything else.

That night, we spent the night under the stars in sleeping bags. Late into the night (or the early morning!) hundreds of young people to the north, south, east and west of us sang native songs and chants to serenade us to sleep. And God blessed us too with a dry and calm night with only the dew to slightly wet us. In the misty morning, myself and another Irish priest went to register to concelebrate the Mass. We made our way across throngs of people towards the sacristy tents. We were told to be there: 'Avant 8h 30' ,as the priest I asked in French told me. We left to go over towards the vesting tents arriving about 7.30 am to be sure to be sure and again, being Irish and being not great at getting up in the morning, we were at the end of long queues that were forming away back from the vesting tents. Eventually we got there and got WYD stoles. All the souvenir chasubles were gone as there was such a dash for them; I saw small priests vested in chasubles trailing off the muddy ground and big priests in 'mini-chasubles'! There was a huge rush for the remaining spoils, but I didn't do too badly. I met up with Capuchin Brothers Robert and Denis from the Australian province who each got a stole along with me. We were directed straight away to the altar area where we waited until the Mass was to begin. We were told that at least 300,000 more people arrived in the morning for the Mass. So now there were more than a million people in Marienfeld eagerly waiting for Pope Benedict XVI to arrive. The high gantry cameras were sweeping along the cranes all over the place to let the millions of viewers at home see the throngs of people gathering in prayer and song to see the new pope begin Mass at 10 am.

MASS WITH THE NEW POPE

The altar was constructed on top of a mound and the canopy was lit up to look like a cloud. The priests were gathered along the foot of the altar mound, a little like the way they had it arranged in the Phoenix Park in 1979. The bishops and cardinals were all to sit around the altar. Many of them were taking photos to remember the huge crowds that gathered to see the pope at the culmination of his first apostolic voyage to his native Germany. At last the entrance procession made its way toward the altar and the pope came along again in the popemobile, waving to people on his left and right. Memories of Pope John Paul II came flooding back, and although Pope Benedict XVI is a different man from his 'superstar' predecessor, he managed to win over the young people of the world as he began the Mass and listened to the words of welcome from Cardinal Meisner of Cologne.

ANYONE WHO HAS DISCOVERED CHRIST MUST LEAD OTHERS TO HIM

During his homily Pope Benedict XVI spoke in German, English, French, Spanish and Italian about how Jesus' crucifixion transforms brutal suffering into an act of self-giving love. Jesus' suffering and death is the victory of love over hatred. The bread and wine are transformed into the body and blood of Christ and we become part of this as the Body of Christ. He asked the young people to remember to keep Sunday a special day. 'It is good that today, in many cultures, Sunday is a free day, and is often combined with Saturday so as to constitute a 'weekend' of free time. Yet this free time is empty if God is not present. Dear Friends! Sometimes, our initial impression is that having to include time for Mass on a Sunday is rather inconvenient. But if you make the effort, you will realise that this is what gives a proper focus to your free time. This is because the Eucharist releases the joy that we need so much, and we need to grasp it ever more deeply, we must learn to love it.'

We were asked to give out Holy Communion and each communion priest was accompanied to a special point all around the vast concourse. We left the ciboria in the specially set-up marquee to be attended to by special ministers of the Eucharist and other priests. We were told not to come back to the altar area for security purposes and to go back for the end of the Mass to our groups. I awaited the final blessing and the Pope's Angelus address from my far-away vantage point courtesy of the big screens again.

LET US GO FORWARD WITH CHRIST

Veterans of WYD always looked forward to this moment at the end of the Angelus address as they used to always anticipate Pope John Paul II making a new appointment with the young people to meet him again as he announced the next international gathering. Poignantly, in Toronto in 2003, John Paul didn't make a new appointment, except to say; 'The next World Youth Day will be in Cologne, Germany in 2005 and Jesus himself will lead you ... '. It was a bittersweet moment for all who were in Toronto and were now gathered in Cologne, because many felt that John Paul was perhaps alluding to the fact that he might not be around. And there were also rumours that Pope Benedict would discontinue WYD in the format that it existed in. However, the new pope, a great admirer and respecter of John Paul II, spoke up in excellent English: 'And I am pleased to announce the next World Youth Day will take place in Sydney, Australia, in 2008.'

So, there's the next appointment of the Holy Father with the young people of the world. And many pundits were saying that this gathering at Marienfeld would be 'The benchmark of the papacy of Benedict XVI', and 'He'd never have the charisma of John Paul II', and 'He's not the consummate showman that JPII was'. Pope Benedict will not be another John Paul II, but Cologne was a great success. Marienfeld was a massive success. The young people all bade farewell to the Pope by chanting 'Benedetto! Benedetto!' Millions saw it on television. I was there and let no one say that young people don't care. After the fall out of the child sexual abuse scandals and the possibility of people being called to account for these evil acts in the future, the Church remains and is in safe hands with these young people. And with over a million young people coming to pray together and to give praise to Jesus Christ the Lord, along with a 78-year-old man who happens to the pope, I am reminded of Jesus' words to the disciples in the Gospel of Matthew (Matthew 28:19ff): 'Go make disciples of all nations, baptise them in the name of the Father, and of the Son, and of the Holy Spirit ... and know that I am with you always, yes to the end of time.'

IN THE AFTERGLOW OF COLOGNE

We left Marienfeld and walked for four hours to the coaches and once we got on the coaches, word reached us that the city was more or less in lockdown due to what some said was a bomb scare. The police were very visible and active and had many roads closed off. We finally left the city and headed north to the frontier and took a wrong turn, so eventually we got to Calais via the Netherlands and Belgium. At Calais there was a delay due to British Customs asking why there were some non-EU people on the coach (some young Australians travelled with us). I remember getting off the coach at Calais and my legs had more or less seized up with pain and tiredness. It took me a while to walk up and down just to get them working again. We made the 4.15 am sailing for Dover and on overland to Holyhead with little time to spare to make the noon sailing to Dun Laoghaire.

I got back to the family home in Kingswood where I must have slept for 12 hours. The whole WYD experience did me good and it was a great chance for me to renew my enthusiasm and my faith in God. For me to witness more than a million people praying together, both over the week of World Youth Day, and at the final Mass with Pope Benedict XVI, and to concelebrate Mass with a pope is not something one does every day, and to hear him preach the Good News to all of us is a bit special to say the least.

The experience of Café Cappuccino too, was something that reminded me why I am at home in the Capuchin Order. To meet with friars from all around the world, who share the same vocation and who live the same rule as me, was also a great support to me.

TOWARDS TODAY AND FLYING!

Just after Christmas 2006, I was given a present of a flying lesson. I have always been very interested in aviation and perhaps this is because my dad brought me to Dublin Airport when other kids were being brought to Parnell or Croke Park.

As I have previously said, I spent much of the summer of 2005 alongside the main runway at Dublin. In fact, I spot planes in Dublin whenever I'm home. I have also spotted planes in Shannon, Cork, London, Paris, Rome and other European airports. Taking flying lessons was something that I often thought about but never got around to. I just needed a little push.

So, there I was, in late January 2006 up at Atlantic Flying School at Cork Airport complete with my voucher. I met the pilot who was going to take me out on my first flying lesson. What an experience! It was a beautiful morning and we flew down over West Cork and back in over the city. It was an opportunity too to take some great photos of the landscape below and the view into the distance. When EI-DDX, a Cessna 172, landed, I knew that I would be interested in continuing – if at all possible.

BACK TO THE PRESENT

I actually ended up doing 42 flying lessons up into the early summer of 2007. Deep down, I knew that while I enjoyed the experience along the way, I was never meant to be a pilot. Early on, I wondered about getting the private pilot's licence (PPL) and being able to fly a plane, but as time went on, I knew that I couldn't give the proper commitment in my world. I was transferred to Dublin in August 2007 and I did give some thought to keeping the flying lessons up, but it wasn't realistic. Flying is a passion, and whether one flies privately or whether one is a career pilot with an airline, it is something that needs time, commitment and hard slog. All of the flying academies aim to be second-to-none today in preparing first-class pilots for the industry. I keep in touch with some friends who are professional pilots flying jets and turboprops and

I've been lucky to have been invited to fly jump seat in the flight deck a few times.

I remember getting a phone call from a friend who now flies Boeing 757's from Dublin across to the east coast of the USA. She was captain on the ATR 72-600s at the time. 'Would I like a trip to Glasgow in the jump seat?' The jump seat is the seat behind the pilots in the flight deck. 'Absolutely!' It was an early Sunday morning flight. We took off on the northerly runway from Dublin and headed up the east coast of Ireland and across to Scotland over Prestwick. We landed in Glasgow and disembarked the passengers and took on the waiting passengers for Dublin. Thirty minutes later we were climbing out and heading back to Dublin. I was back in Dublin and back in the car and on the altar in Halston Street for the 12 pm Mass to tell the people of my adventure that morning. Incidentally, they were going over to Glasgow and back again after I left.

On the few occasions when I do fly in a plane, I imagine what the pilots are doing up on the flight deck, especially as it taxis to the runway threshold. On the take-off roll, the engines are powered up to full throttle and that's when we get pushed into the seatback. I imagine the pilots working together saying '80 knots' as the aircraft gains speed. Automatically the plane will tell the pilots when it has reached 'V-one' speed. This is the speed at which the pilot must decide to continue the take-off or stop within the safe distance. The pilot calls out 'rotate' and pulls back on the control column or the side stick and the nose is raised into the air. The pilot then calls 'positive climb' and the co-pilot calls 'gear up', and the landing gear is cleaned up and stowed away till before landing. All the while the pilots are talking to air traffic control (ATC), and being handed over to another controller along the way. Most of the flight is handled by the automatic pilot, where the pilots feed in the height and compass heading to the autopilot each time ATC issues an instruction, and the plane flies itself.

Up there in a plane it's nice to know that each pilot, even cosmonauts and astronauts who came in to the space agencies from the air force, and who orbit the earth in the ISS, all began their flying careers in Cessnas, Pipers, Grobs and other light aircraft. As a boy, I used to spot planes along the old runway 06/23 in Dublin Airport and there were many others there too. Judging by the numbers of people stopping along the runways today, and the people who are members of social media airline enthusiasts' groups, planes still fascinate many people.

Fifty

I'm looking at a black-and-white photo of myself as a little baby. My mother tells me I was 14 weeks old in it, so judging by that, it is the beginning of 1970. I notice he is looking up at someone or something, his big blue eyes are wide, and his eyebrows are raised. He has a crocheted poncho shawl and little socks. He looks like he's in good form. His left arm and hand are reaching up and out and this may be a hint to his growing up a ciotóg, or left-handed. He is sitting in his baby seat and it fits very well into the armchair. He seems to be listening intently and paying attention

He would grow up the eldest of seven siblings during the 1970s and 1980s. A baby photo would be taken again over the years for another two boys and four girls. Each child would be loved and even spoiled at times, even when times were hard and there was little money. That little baby would grow up with the other ones and we would live in a happy home. We would know the difference between right and wrong and we would know where we stood when it came to the crunch. I think he gave good example and he remembers being reminded that as the first-born, he would be expected to act as the leader. 'You're the eldest, you shouldn't have allowed them to make a mess.' I mean, it was very difficult to stop four, five and then six brothers and sisters from turning the house upside-down on a wet Saturday morning in the 1980s. We had only a few stations on the Ferguson television set back then, and of course there were no smartphones and no WiFi. Like most of the neighbours, the telephone was on the phone table at the bottom of the stairs and my mother put on her telephone accent when she came to the phone. The whole house was our playground on a wet weekend, and it got messy. I remember drawing aeroplanes on the steamy windowpane when the dinner was being cooked. Mam was always there at home. Most mothers were at home when we were kids. She would be dozing in her chair with the orange cushions by the fire, a real coal fire, when we would come in from school, and while her eyes were closed, we would tell her about our day. She would have finished all her housework and the baby would be asleep. 'Shhh.' We would soon make more work for her and more noise to wake the baby. What's for dinner? Crispy pancakes, potatoes and peas. TK Ciderette.

Homework would be put off on a bad day, and on a good day it would be done on the kitchen table after dinner. It is not something I like to remember. As I write, the Leaving Certificate exams begin today. I sat the Leaving Cert in June 1987, 32 years ago this year. I used a blue pen with 'Padre Pio pray for us' written on it. I was planning on joining the Capuchins in September. I remember very little about that exam except the warm June days on the fourth floor of the school. I looked blankly at the Maths paper and three decades later I still don't know where to begin. I know the words 'sin', 'cos' and 'tan', but that's where it ends.

I didn't like school, although I do have some happy memories here and there. I went to three different primary schools growing up because we moved house in the 1970s and early 1980s. Myself and my brother Kevin, a year and 11 months younger, who is now deputy principal in a community school and a married father of three, went to the same schools and we were one school year apart. We share the same memories and stories of our school days. The others, Gráinne, David, Aoife, Lorna and Clodagh, came along after.

I am grateful to God for growing up in a close family and, while we have our moments, I'd be lost without them.

I would argue that going to school in Ireland in the 1970s and early 1980s was almost completely different from what school students experience today. There was corporal punishment then and I was slapped like most of the lads at the time in primary school. While I did misbehave and disruptive behaviour meant being hit at times, one of the things that I found horrible was being blamed for someone else's wrongdoing.

For example, being put 'outside the door' meant you ran the risk of being caught by the principal and that meant being slapped with the 'leather'; a strap made of hardened leather with metal coins on the inside and stitched together. One day we were in the school hall during PE and a group of us were sitting on the floor watching a five-a-side indoor football game. The next thing I remember was five or six of us on the floor in a heap. Two other lads jumped on top of us when the teacher wasn't looking. He turned towards us all, pointed to us and said; 'One, two, three, four, five; outside the door.' And we were put out, the guilty and the innocent. The teacher changed his mind and brought us back in after a few minutes and gave us a warning. But had we stayed outside, and had the principal come along, it probably would have meant 'getting the leather'.

When the door was open, we could hear the sound of someone being hit all the way up the corridors. The floors were that freezing terrazzo with a rock-hard surface, and everything boomed and echoed. If it wasn't the leather, it was a stick, or a broom handle or a piece of cane. We used to warm our hands off the radiators before being hit. You'd see some lads rubbing their hands off their legs and knees. Once the slaps were administered, we would try to cool the stinging and throbbing on the cold bars of the desks and on cold days it would hurt more. My Nana used to say when they were kids, they would lick the palms of their hands, take a hair from their head, and put it on the centre of the palm which meant it didn't hurt as much. I tried this and it made no difference!

Another thing that I feel was very unfair was using punishment as a vehicle to make you learn something. One day the teacher never showed up in class and the principal (in order to keep us quiet) stood at the door and told us he was going to come back in 15 minutes and give us an oral test. We were to learn our maths tables and he would test us on the division tables. He said it would be a quick-fire test and those who didn't know the answers … well … naturally we swotted away for those 15 minutes and there wasn't a sound. By then another teacher had come in and that was an answer to prayer.

Sometimes going home from primary school, we would walk along the old canal by the flats. The Luas Red Line runs along that route now and it is almost a world away from what it used to be. Some of the lads from the flats, lads we were in school with, would stop us and there would be a skirmish. There would be fisticuffs and swearing and crying and 'I'll tell me Ma on you.' One time, a lad used a Stanley knife to cut the side of my Manchester United school bag. My Nana had bought it for me the day before. My dad went to the school to complain about this. I can't remember what happened or if the lad was punished. My dad stitched it together with steel wire. Another time, lads I knew took my markers from my school bag, two of them held me down and drew on my face! I went home with red eyes and my mother said; 'What happened to you?' 'Nothing,' I said.

Some of the lads were featured in a *Today Tonight* special on the flats. It told the story of poverty, unemployment and the emerging drug problem in some of these corporation flat complexes. It also spoke of the great work that many people were trying to do on the ground to make a difference and today that work has largely paid dividends. In the programme, while filming one morning, one of the community volunteers takes the camera crew down to the boiler house in the basement of one of the flats complex and there they find some of the young lads hiding out or 'mitching from school'. In our glossary, we referred to mitching, or playing truant, as being 'on the hop'. When the RTÉ presenter asked the lads why they were weren't in school one of them said, 'We hate the bleedin' yoke'. The next day in school we were all talk and excitement about our mitching classmates.

In fifth year in secondary school a few lads misbehaved in Irish class. For a punishment, the teacher drafted a letter of apology for each of them and they had to read it out to the class one by one. I remember being embarrassed for them as there were one or two wouldn't have been in the ranks of the 'messers'. I look back on it now as it being an exercise in humiliation for them in front of us all.

When I was in sixth year, months before I joined the order, a school football team was leaving on the school bus to play a match. Some of the lads were shouting their good luck out the windows of the school. I remember looking out the window myself and shouting good luck too. When I turned around, the principal was standing there almost in my face. I copped the silence in the classroom just that little bit too late. He had forbidden lads opening windows up on the fourth floor. I imagine he was fearful of an accident or insurance. In a split second, I uttered something like 'What's the problem?' He hit me across the back of the head and the whole class witnessed it. One of my classmates told me later that the class captain should have come to my defence by saying I wasn't well and was getting fresh air!

This principal had an interesting way of punishing lads. He would stand us outside in the middle of the yard as an example to everyone else. He ordered me to do just that. I had to stay standing in the yard although I moved towards the sheds next to the PE Hall. Luckily, I only had half an hour to go and I packed my bags and went home. There was no more about it after that in that I'm not sure if he ever noticed me again in school.

I can't leave some of the memories of my schooldays without acknowledging that while I had some teachers I didn't particularly like, I also admit that in a few cases I probably tried the patience of some of them in primary and secondary school. However, there were some very fine teachers, lay teachers and Christian Brothers, who were committed, kind, and good educators. I remember three Christian Brothers, two who taught me, and hand on heart, I know they believed in us boys and were very affirming. I am grateful to them for lots of reasons. Edmund Rice would be proud of men like these for to me they encapsulated the spirit he tried to establish in giving of their talents, skills and expertise, and seeking no reward.

I am friendly to this day with one or two of the lay teachers I had in secondary school, and one, in particular, contacts me from time to time with news and updates from the school and the past pupils' union. He always encouraged me, and I didn't know this at the time, but he often told other teachers that I would make a great priest. I hope I'm living up to this.

My schooldays are going further and further back into the distance but through social media I have linked up with a lot of the old schoolfriends. Many of us met in 2017 on the periphery of our year group's 30th anniversary. It was as if some of us hadn't left the school at all and we spent the whole evening talking about the past and telling stories of adventures we had in school. What I didn't know was that one of the lads present that night was unwell and had battled with bad health for quite a while. Shortly after we were all together, news came through that he had died. He was only 47. The family asked me to preach the homily at his funeral Mass and later, as I reflected on his passing, I realised that already, two lads from our class have died since we left in June 1987.

I write this chapter as I approach my 50th birthday. Many say that it is a milestone. Fifty years is a golden jubilee and a half-century. When I was a boy, my grandparents were in their 50s and to us kids, they were old. The Capuchins who celebrated their golden jubilees when I was a student friar were eminent men, and the diamond jubilarians were really old. Today, many have reached their 70th anniversaries, so people are living much longer now. For me, pushing 50, I can't escape it because already I've been at some friends' 50th birthdays and there are more on the way. How do I feel about my own? I'm not worried about being 50 or about getting old but perhaps that will change as I head for 60 and older.

1969 was a year when some big and famous things happened. The first flight of the Boeing 747 Jumbo jet, today known as 'the Queen of the Skies', took place on 9 February. The first test-flight of the BAC/Aerospatiale Concorde was on 2 March that year. On 21 July, Commander Neil Armstrong became to first man to walk on the Moon followed by Col. Edwin 'Buzz' Aldrin. The famous outdoor concert at Woodstock, from 15 to 18 August, attracted 350,000 rock-and-roll fans. In Ireland, Jack Lynch was taoiseach, and Eamon de Valera was president. Richard Nixon replaced Lyndon Johnson as president of the USA. Harold Wilson was the British prime minister and Elizabeth II was the sovereign. In the Vatican, Paul VI was pope. In Poland, Cardinal Karol Wojtyla was Archbishop of Krakow and in South America, a Jesuit scholastic from Argentina called Jorge Bergoglio was ordained priest.

I've probably lived half my life. When I see some references to the government's future plans, for example, 'Project Ireland 2040', I think – if I'm around then, I will be 79. I was chatting to my dad recently and he was talking about my nephews and nieces, the grandchildren. The eldest grandson will be 18 years old later this year. The youngest grandson is five months old, and my dad quipped that he would be 96 when the baby reaches 18. There was a NASA astronaut on one of the Irish daytime radio talk shows a few years ago. He was over for a speaking engagement in the University of Limerick and I seem to remember one of the things he said was that the first men and women who will go to Mars are young people right now. Next year another Mars Rover will be launched which will take 11 months to travel to the Red Planet. I imagine we are still decades away from manned flights to Mars. NASA is planning to go back to the moon by 2024. So, Armstrong's famous words broadcast all over the world as he stepped onto the surface of the Moon, 'One small step for man, one giant leap for mankind', is still very much a work in progress today. That summer, my mother, a young married woman, expecting her first baby in October, was advised to rest and not to stay up late to watch the astronauts landing on the moon. She stayed up and witnessed what everyone else watched that night. Funny, she used to sing us lullabies when we were tiny, and I remember this one, which perhaps is appropriate to close this chapter on:

Lulla-lulla Lulla-lulla bye-bye;
Do you want the moon to play with?
Or the stars to run away with?
They'll come if you don't cry ...

Lulla-lulla bye-bye;
In your mammy's arms a-creepin'
And soon you'll be asleep, a-singing
Lulla-Lulla bye ...

Seraphic Humour

OVERHEARD IN THE FRIARY

You might remember there was a popular book published some years ago called *Overheard on the Luas*. It illustrated how people can hear all sorts of humour contained in the conversations of Dublin commuters on the Luas lines. I began to think of putting together some of the humour I've overheard through the years in the Capuchins and also hilarious stories that friars have heard and told.

We friars are together a lot because we are a family. We pray together and eat together and sit together in the community room in the evenings at the end of the day. In recent times, some of the challenges to community life (as it is for all family life) is social media and smartphones, as many of us have the mobile phones nearby. I've noticed some use their phones or tablets to read the Psalms or the Scriptures or the Office of Readings from the Breviary.

When we are together, like all families we will recall stories, crack jokes, and remember many of the friars who have died who made a big impact on the community. A lot of them are referred to by their nicknames. One of the friars who taught in the university was referred to as 'the Doc' or 'the Prof'. We had a man who was known as 'Tombstone', another, Apollinaris, was called 'Polly'. We even had a man who everyone called 'the Sheriff'.

At meals the conversations would be lively, stories would be told, and men who have died would be brought back to life around the table. I've lived in 12 communities since I joined the order in 1987 and I've some amazing memories.

When we were novices, we experienced our first Christmas dinner in a friary. The table was heavy with food and all the friars from 19 to 85 years of age sat down to celebrate Christmas Day after the morning Masses. You name it, it was there: starter, soup, main course, dessert, minerals and wine. One of the friars noticed that 'there's not a banana in sight!' When we were student friars in Dublin, one of the members of the community used to go all out to help celebrate Christmas. The community room and refectory would be decked with lights and tinsel. The tables would be pushed to the centre of the room and we would all sit around with paper hats and Christmas crackers. We even had a train set in the centre of the table with the engine going round and round. The guardian of the friary, one of the nicest friars I have ever known, used to make sure each member of the community would receive a little gift and we would all take turns opening them.

I remember one of the men I lived with loved his food. He would fill his plate up high with spuds, vegetables and meat. The man who sat across from him used to get amused with the big helpings. One day he wasn't in at dinner time and the man opposite looked at the empty place and quipped; 'There must be good grazing elsewhere today.' Another time I remember each time a dish came to the table one of the friars used to give a running commentary; 'Soup... Soup...' 'Chicken ... Chicken ... ', 'Potatoes ... Potatoes ... ', 'Carrots ... Carrots ... '. It came to the dessert. 'Queen of Puddings ... Queen of Puddings ...' One friar replied, 'Pray for us!'

During Holy Week, we were praying the Psalms of the Evening Prayer of Monday (Week 2). We were all gathered together in the chapel and one of the older friars, who had been bursar for many years was to recite the first antiphon: 'He had no beauty, no majesty to draw our eyes, no grace to make us delight in him.' When he came to read what came out instead was; 'He had no money ... '. One of the other friars began to laugh out loud and immediately it set us all off and the evening prayer had to be abandoned. Today, all we have to do is say 'he had no money' and we still chuckle.

Here are some of the things that have been 'overheard' in the friary in the past few years; it is a small flavour of what I call 'Seraphic Humour':

* * *

'I want to take the pledge for life.'

'Maybe take it for a few months first.'

'Sure – I always take it for life.'

* * *

'That's a great shop on Dawson Street; Pen Corner. You know who owns it of course?'

'No.'

'His Nibs.'

* * *

'Will you have a little after-dinner drink?'

'I'll have a Grand Marnier, we always had that at home in West Cork.'

* * *

A visiting monk; 'I joined the order in '62 and finished my studies and was ordained in '71. I missed the Beatles!'

* * *

'There's a new café on Henry Street.'

'What part of Henry Street is it on?'

''Tis on one side if you go down.'

* * *

'In the past the friars' greeting to each other was; "Pax et Bonum".

Now it's "Fax et Phone- 'em". '

* * *

'If I were you, I'd watch him closely from a distance.'

* * *

'Yeah, he'd be known as an apostate ... '
'That would have something to do with the gland then ... eh?'

* * *

'Brother; did you ever dance?'
'No!'
'But I bet you made other friars dance.'

* * *

Two friars talking about a 'larger' friar walking slowly past the church.
'Look at him – the one-man procession.'

* * *

'That's the first nun I ever saw with an iPad.'
'Why? Was there something wrong with her eye?'

* * *

'Did St John of the Cross's 'Dark Night of the Soul' happen during the day? '

* * *

'Who put the teabag in the collection plate?'

* * *

'Brother, when you advance in age, there's only memory lanes.'

* * *

(in the car park) 'Back away; there's nothing in front of you.'

* * *

'That fella would start an argument in an empty room.'

* * *

'What's the WiFi code?'

* * *

Two friars talking about the anniversary of a friar on this day.

'Do you remember did old Brother N, his fellow novice, go to the cemetery for the prayers?'

'No, he didn't. He said if he went it wouldn't be worth his while coming back.'

* * *

'How is Brother N?'

'Oh, he's not too well.'

'And how is Brother M?'

'He's not well either.'

'See, that's the way it is today, it's not e-bay any more – it's sick-bay.'

* * *

'Some fellas like Gaelic games, or soccer games, but he prefers mind-games.'

Philomena Lynott, RIP[4]

I first met Philomena Lynott in Cork around 2005, although of course I had known of her for a long time. She was staying with Edel in Connolly Road and Edel rang me one Saturday evening and said, 'Her Maj is here and would love to meet you.' I was based in our friary in Rochestown at the time. When I arrived, I was dressed in my Franciscan habit and Philomena was introduced to me as 'Father Bryan'. She didn't know what to make of me. There are no airs and graces with Edel, and I made myself at home. Edel said to me, 'The kettle is boiled, go out and make yourself a cup of tea.' When I went into the kitchen, I could hear Philomena say to Edel, 'Is he really a priest? When he came in the door, I thought he was in fancy dress!'

In 2007, I was transferred to work as chaplain in Beaumont Hospital. One evening on duty I recognised Philomena coming down the corridor. She was visiting her beloved Denis who was a patient there at the time. She greeted me, 'Oh, how are you? You're Edel's friend!' And later she phoned Edel to say she had met her friend and he really is a priest! She often reminded me of this when I met her again.

In the context of this funeral Mass this morning, some images come to mind when I think of Philomena. She was a mother who genuinely put people first. She lived her life at the service of others, despite the difficulties and struggles that came along.

Certainly, we all know of her devotion to her beloved Philip. In the

4   Homily I gave at Philomena's Funeral Mass – 17 June 2019.

last 33 years, she made sure that his legacy as an artist, a musician, and a poet was firmly passed on. All across the world so many people loved his music and he was like a bridge between genres; Rock, Pop, Folk, Punk and the New Wave. Philip Lynott was a pioneer to many that came after him. His mam helped in passing on the message.

She always had time for the fans and so many felt comfortable coming up the driveway of White Horses and all were welcome. In fact, Philip and Lizzy were slow to refer to their legions of fans as fans. They were their 'supporters' and Philomena made sure to honour them.

I am reminded of the U2 song, 'Iris' from the album *Innocence + Experience*. Bono speaks eloquently of his mother who died before her time: 'I've got your life inside of me.' When a child is born, the mother passes on the light to them. We grow up carrying their love and light inside and it shows every time we reach out to one another. Philip died before his mother and it was as if she guarded that light again for him and passed it on.

When Philip died, Philomena was heartbroken. I see the image of Mary the mother of Jesus here in a sense. Mary who told us to do what her son tells us and then we see the miracles happen. Mary who suffered as Jesus did. Philomena devoted herself to visiting his grave and tending the flowers there. Now, of course Irish mammies are best placed to administer tough love. They want the best for their kids. Philomena wasn't afraid to tell us that she was crushed and hurt when Philip died a young man. She made it her life's work to be that mammy to so many others and to highlight the dangers and the mirage that the entertainment industry can sometimes be for some. She talked of giving Phil's gravestone a 'good kick' for what he did to her ... But it was always because she loved him so much. I believe I heard the rumble of thunder last Wednesday when she passed. I was chatting to my brother Kevin and he said that when Philomena got to the gates of heaven, Jesus called Philip over, put his arm around him and said; 'Guess who just got back today ... ?' When Philomena saw Philo, I'm sure sparks flew up there. She was a force of nature.

So, we bring her to her place of rest today. She will keep a good eye on him now. But she will keep an eye on all of us and make sure we pass on the light going forward. In the song 'Philomena, which he wrote for his mammy, Philip says; 'If you see my mother, please give her all my love. For she has a heart of gold there. As good as God above ... '. He has seen her over the years as she spread that love. Now, she sees him again and what a reunion it must be.

Philomena, may the angels lead you into paradise,
May the saints take you by the hand,
And walk with you into the presence of God. Amen.

Down to Nana's

I clearly remember the day my mother sent myself and my brother Kevin on the bus for the first time on our own. We must have been nearly nine and nearly 11 years old. We got the 19A bus from the County Bar in Rialto village to the National Boxing Stadium on the South Circular Road. It was a short trip as the bus went on into town as we called it and out over to the north side. I remember it must have been the summer as we weren't in school. We generally went down to our Nana's on Tuesday and Saturday afternoons. This was more or less a routine all my life s.

Mam coached us as to what to say as we boarded the bus, a CIE black-and-white Atlantean type bus. 'Two halves to the Stadium please.' 'He will let you out beside the Spar,' she said. The memories are coming back as I write. The hiss of the doors as we got on. The black and grey flecked floor-covering. The blue rope bell that went along the ceiling and the button bell on the wall with the instruction to 'push once'. In those days there were bus conductors with a silver ticket machine which printed the chit on blue ink in Irish and English. The smell of the ticket paper was the same smell as the paper that wrapped up the fish and chips. They also had a leather satchel with the money in it to give back the change. If downstairs was full you would hear the conductor announce, 'Seats on the top.' There was no smoking downstairs, but people were allowed to smoke upstairs on the bus. The thick stench of smoke found its way onto everyone's clothes. On a wet day, the smell of cigarettes on the upper deck seemed to be more toxic and even sticky. In the 21st century it is almost impossible to imagine that people were allowed to smoke on buses, trains and even in aircraft once upon a time. Perhaps in the future it will even be hard to imagine that at one time people smoked.

Myself and Kevin travelled the five stops or so up to Dolphin's Barn and along the South Circular Road by the old Player Wills cigarette factory and up to the Stadium. We got off the bus at the Spar and walked down Greenville Terrace, around onto Dufferin Avenue, on to Petrie Avenue and to O'Curry Road. Mam followed along later, and Dad would meet us there after work.

We arrived at No. 33 and blew into my poor Nana's house. Herself and our grandfather, we called him Grandpop or 'Grampop', were sitting by the fire. The fire would be lit off the embers of last night's fire. He would be smoking his pipe filled with Condor tobacco and she would be smoking John Player Red. He would be waiting on the *Evening Press* newspaper to be delivered into the letter box where he would glance at the headlines but quickly get stuck into crossword. He had a well-thumbed copy of the Collins Gem Dictionary in the press to his left hand. Their cat, Cola, would be looking for her ears to be scratched while purring loudly. Grampop would be called for his dinner and he would sit up from his armchair and sit at the table. Lamb chops and peas and buttery mashed potatoes. Tinned pears or peaches and custard or ice-cream for dessert. When I was very small, Nana's bachelor brother, Tommy, lived in the house. He was known as Uncle Me-Me. He had a nickname for me and Kevin. I was Johnny Banger and Kevin was 'Two Ton'. He died not long after my sister Gráinne was born. He sat over on his own armchair and read the paper and often compared notes with Grampop.

At Nana's there was a picture of the Sacred Heart on the wall, as in many homes in the past. The family would be consecrated to the Sacred Heart of Jesus and signed by the priest. Nana would burn a little lamp under the picture and I'm sure she remembered all of us in prayer each day. It is probably fair to say that nearly all grandchildren love their grandparents. Someone said that God couldn't be everywhere so that's why he created grandmothers. The Catholic Grandparent's Association holds St Joachim and St Anne, the parents of Our Lady, as patrons and also Louis and Zélie Martin, the recently canonised parents of St Thérèse of Lisieux. I am confident that my four grandparents are in heaven and the main reason I believe this is that they passed on the faith, no questions asked, to our parents. Also, Pope Francis had a great love for his grandparents and often holds up grannies and granddads as models of faith.

Nana's masterpiece was her stew. I think Irish grannies will be remembered for generations for the ability to make something out of nothing and therefore feed the neighbourhood, and also for the flavour of their stews and coddle. Our mam will readily agree that she could never quite get the hang of the unique flavour of her mother's stew and coddle. I can still taste every bit of it, and it is almost sacramental to me. There was goodness, and love and generosity in it.

Nana was a natural grandmother, with stories and tales of her own childhood. She grew up in tough times where there was very little money and those in authority really were in authority, state and Church. It was hard to be a young person and a young married couple in the 1930s and 1940s. We look from the prism of today and all that we have in our lives in terms of progress and technology. But in our Nana's day, and even in our mother's day, life was often hard. Nana's sister, Auntie Chrissie, had an old friend who was a member of the Church of Ireland. Chrissie attended her funeral service even though it was forbidden at the time for a Catholic to enter a Protestant Church. That rule seems so crazy today, yet Chrissie was afraid to tell the priest she went to the funeral. Thank God those days are gone. When I read of old Dublin and old Ireland, I thank God that we learned about it while sitting on her knee and not just in the schoolroom.

Our dad would pull up outside around 6 pm in his red Mini Traveller or his Renault 12. He had a special type of knock which is hard to describe in writing. It was that classic tune ending; 'Shave-and-a-haircut. Bay Rum.' Or the Ronnie Drew version; 'How-is-your-auld'-wan? - game-ball.' He would come in, pipe in his mouth, and have a fill (a smoke) with Grampop and soon we'd be piled into the car, no seatbelts, because there were no seatbelts, and back home again. When we lived in Kilnamanagh, near Tallaght, we'd stop at the shops for smokes for my mother on the way. And this was the routine as we grew up.

Nana died in February 1991. She was still relatively young at 74 years old. While she hadn't been well, we never really wanted to believe she would die. She worried about death and, as did many God-fearing people of her generation; some priests filled their people with more scruples than mercy. Week in and week out, she and Grampop went to Mass and even met Mother St Theresa of Calcutta on the street in the parish where she lived. She baptised her children, my mother and my aunts, and brought them up to believe in God. They did the same for us. All their lives Nana and Grampop, Granny Gretta and Grandad practised their faith, and yet many of their generation lived with some fear that God was not a god of mercy and forgiveness. She introduced me to St Padre Pio, who she loved, and we walked years later up to the Irish Office for Padre Pio which was on Dufferin Avenue until 2018. Nana often said to me that when she died and she met Jesus, she would grab on to his tunic and hold on tight to him so he couldn't let her go (to hell?). I'm angry even writing this. How dare any church or priest lay that burden on a person who, in great difficulty and with a hard life, kept the faith and did so with a sense of humour, even when some in authority tried to rob her spirit. They, the ordinary Irish parents, were a heroic generation who built our Republic. She's looking down on me now and I hear her voice through my tears from the kingdom. I'll see you down the road, Nana – you all. I've never been more certain you're all in heaven.

Epilogue

'IT'S SUCH A WASTE!'

We loved the monthly teenage disco. We'd excitedly count down the days in eager anticipation and talk about little else during the week it was on. If you were lucky, you might even have had the money in the lead-up to buy that lemon short-sleeved shirt with grey epaulettes and pockets in Penneys. It could go really well with your grey flecked trousers and red side-laced shoes while you queued up in the evening sun at the door, with your 50 pence entrance fee in hand, parading yourself in front of your peers and potential girlfriends.

During the summer projects, the teenage discos took place in the local boy's school hall, which was a rare parish dispensation. During the rest of year, about a hundred of us were transferred on an overcrowded 53-seater coach to a neighbouring estate, because we weren't allowed to use the local school hall for discos. Going elsewhere on a bus, while logistically more difficult to organise for the committee, was great fun and it was more exciting travelling there and back. But the ones during the summer were the best. They were longer, more people went and you could stay out later. Everyone spent more time together during the day too in the summer so the preparation and preoccupation was electric. You might have had a bit of sunburn that evening from the day's excursion to Clara Lara Fun Park or Brittas Bay, more than the odd person still had muck on their knees or sand in their hair that evening in the queue. Usually though, when you got back from the day trip, there was just enough time to get home, get dinner and change into the lemon shirt. Nowadays we'd shower. Back then Lynx Oriental or Blue Stratos body spray and Galaxy hair gel substituted for a shower and covered a multitude.

Bryan loved the discos, he had an encyclopaedic knowledge of music and for the past year had been the DJ too. Not tonight, however, this disco was very different, it was his last one with us. The school hall was packed and warm. The single glazed wooden windows all around were steamed up and deep blue in colour as twilight approached and lit them from behind. The incandescent flashing lights on the inside of the room became more effective and evocative as the room darkened. Initial conversations full of awkwardness, anxiety and inhibition gave way to calmness and equilibrium as the sun weakened and synthetic light dominated. A generation of suburban, late 1980s adolescents filled the floor, lived in the moment and danced like nothing else mattered. Discos in those days were made up of songs and tracks, each one independent, recognisable and finished before the next started. There was always a steady flow of girls and boys leaning over the desk at the top of the hall, where the turntables were, trying to attract the attention of the busy, dancing, gum-chewing DJ to make a request; and the majority of requests related to and hastened the central ritual of the evening.

The 'slow set' was announced. 'We're gonna slow tings down now,' said the MC in his thick Dublin, mixed with a tinge of bass, mid-Atlantic accent. We all sat down except for those already in relationships, who immediately started to slow dance. 'True Colours', by Cindy Lauper was usually first, or 'Drive', by The Cars. The intro of each number was the perfect start and intimately known by us all as a call to action. They weren't the best or favourite or most central songs to begin with. That title went to Chicago, or Kool and the Gang or Marillion or Jim Diamond or Spandau Ballet. 'Come on Eileen' usually ended the set.

Anyone who went to a disco in the 1980s laments the demise of the slow set. So much has been said and written about it there's no need to describe it further. Those that were there and lived through it, get it, and those that weren't and didn't, won't. Like going on blind dates or arranging to meet at a specific location at a specific time such as Clery's Clock or the Central Bank, or like reciting a telephone number as you answered it – such customs are a focus of sentimental recollection and largely a thing of the past. But one aspect of this slow set time, which was fundamental, ever-present and etched into the memory but far less discussed or written about, is central to this story. It wasn't the separation of the sexes, or the nervous approach when asking someone to dance or the walk of shame when rejected or the wink or the smug face when you got a positive response or when she put her head on your shoulder. It was what happened off the floor, in the margins, where the unlucky ones mixed with those too cool to dance, those who'd finished, those who didn't care or finally those who didn't need to prove themselves. We all pretended we were in the latter group but few truly belonged to it or wanted to be there. It did offer a break from the noise and afforded a chance to talk. Not everything that was said was honest but often it was a time for genuine, inward feelings. It was a lonely time for some.

During the slow set, those not dancing largely adhered to those on the floor with varying or mixed emotions. Some friends would have flippant conversations about a couple on the floor, evaluating their level of seriousness, history and future. Some individuals stood alone silently, awkwardly pretending to read a notice in the distance and examining their fingernails repeatedly. There were no phones to get lost in. Some went out for air or to the toilet. The odd group stood together without talking until the atmosphere was broken by a playful punch on the arm or a scramble for sweets. All the while, in the background, among most groups of both sexes, scheming, plotting and matchmaking was going on and lines of communication were being established to further the numbers pairing off. Now and again some genuine conversations occurred, and interesting or unforgettable comments were made. 'She fancies you, she's not worth it, he doesn't deserve you, he just wants to be friends, it's all off, why is he with her, she's too mature for you?' All these comments are treated as fact and represent the whole world to a 16-year-old at the time. The emotion that accompanies any statement of information remains long after the detail. As you stare at the darkened, silhouetted floor for one reason or another the comment that's whispered in your ear could be turned over countless times in your mind, so much so that the associated sentiments and feelings never leave you. Tonight was one of those nights.

Bryan was dancing with his girlfriend. I watched on. It doesn't matter why I wasn't dancing! 'Cherish' by Kool and the Gang was playing, my favourite. I had never really thought about the words before: 'the world is always changing, nothing stays the same, but love must stand the test of time, the next life that we live in remains to be seen, will you be by my side ... ?'

My world was changing because Bryan's world was really changing, nothing was going to stay the same. Everyone loved Bryan and I was lucky because he was my brother and my best friend. But he was going away to be a priest. In about three weeks' time he was leaving forever. It was an unknown future because, unlike in the past or in different parts of the country or the world, 18-year-old breakdancers from Tallaght didn't join the priesthood. None of us, and when I say 'us' I mean our very large community of friends, had any experience, perspective or precedent for this. No one we ever knew did what Bryan was about to do, but we were aware, even then, of how rare and unusual his choice was. Everyone respected him for it, celebrated it and supported him because he was so popular and well known in the community. He was full of integrity and was nobody's fool, was normal, good looking, honest, very visible, outgoing, sensible and reliable. His friends called him 'Bro'. He transcended different social circles and age groups. His going away was a big story. I was a bit jealous, embarrassed, confused and torn. The song went on: 'If you receive your calling before I awake ...'

I gazed into the distance beyond my original focus. What did that line mean? What 'calling' was the song talking about? Bryan was 18 and I was 16 and I just wondered about the whole lot of it, everything. Was he really called? I didn't trust him, I didn't trust his reasoning, it was typical Bryan. I didn't believe God called him to be a priest, I felt it was as if he let God twist his arm, God got the better of him. He shouldn't have given in. As if the world showed its face to me and I wanted it and couldn't resist it, but Bryan was too good to be fooled by it, was suspicious of my carelessness and was even pig-headed for doing what was right. 'Why was he doing this?' I asked myself. Why couldn't he live in the clouds, like me, with my naïve, blinkered, pie-in-the-sky, unrealistic plan for life, instead of doing something so tangible and outrageously bold?

As I almost blanked out the whole room and processed my secret, internalised questions, I became aware of the smell of perfume beside me. The best-looking girl in the whole estate stood there; she belonged to the latter group of non-dancers who didn't need to prove herself to anyone. She put her arm around me and asked was I OK. I immediately forgot about everything that was on my mind and wondered if I should ask her to dance, but she was about 18 and in those days we were compulsively aware of the subtleties of age difference and who was and wasn't out of our league.

I decided against entertaining the idea of a dance and just said I was OK and was going to miss my brother. What I heard next was another bolt from the blue and put me right back into deep thought. She said, 'I know, it's such a waste.'

I paused and thought about the statement, which I'd heard so many times before from friends and strangers alike in reference to Bryan's future plans. Up to now it had become something of a cliché, a repetitive meaningless statement that had lost its original meaning or intention however inaccurate or offensive its initial iteration. It wasn't really the considered position or sentiments of the person saying it; it was over-said and repeated, just like the stock answer people use when asked about how their Christmas was and they respond by saying, 'It was quiet.' Surely everyone's Christmas isn't quiet, but that's uniformly and consistently how people describe it when asked. This time, when I heard 'It's such a waste', I was overcome with anger and frustration and an overwhelming urge to defend my brother's integrity, but from myself and my darker more negative thoughts. I was all of a sudden guilted into facing my own bias and selfish feelings. Why should I or anyone else question someone's free choice, especially one so difficult, rare and well-intentioned? To my shame I never responded, addressed or challenged the statement then or afterwards. I didn't hear it as much as time went on and I never hear it now, especially from people that know Bryan or anyone from back then.

In the intervening years, friends and people that I met who knew Bryan would always ask about him more than me or anyone else in the family. His choice of lifestyle back then seemingly continued to be as unusual and noteworthy as time went on. Up until about 10 years ago, whenever I met anyone that I knew during our school or disco days, they would always enquire: 'How is Bryan, is he still in the priesthood?' I think this question reflects culture as much as their memories of him. How well known and highly thought of he was, how eventful and newsworthy his vocation was, but probably more accurately, they were cognisant of the decline in vocations to religious life, the waning influence of the Church and the increased incidence of people leaving ministry. Perhaps they expected the bloke they knew growing up would leave also.

Now, more than 30 years on from that summer night, no one I meet ever asks whether my brother is still a priest. I've often wondered why. Is it because he's more well known through his media appearances, his work or his writing and they therefore know he's still at it? Maybe. Or is it because things have quietened down a little in the dialogue and dynamic about the decline of the Church? The public increasingly sees priests as unique and individual rather than institutional, getting on with it but with less of the drama. The Church may not be crumbling any more, i's just smaller, less ubiquitous and in a more stable space to discern its future direction. Is it that Bryan is viewed through this more mature or contemporary lens by his peers and society in general?

I met that perfumed girl from the disco in 1987 recently, she's about 50 now. She didn't ask how Bryan was, she told me he christened three of her children, blessed her sick aunt, buried her dad and how she saw him with the pope on TV, and read about him in *Hot Press*. She told me how she bought his book in Easons and called to him to get it signed. She showed me a selfie of the two of them on her phone. Then she said: 'Ah Bryan, he's great, he's unbelievable, he does great work, not like some of them wasters we knew growing up.'

I thought to myself of her words all those years ago and how she said his life choice was such a waste. It taught me a valuable lesson. Bryan didn't challenge the prevailing view of himself verbally at the time, his life challenged the prevailing stereotypes. He let people say what they wanted and think what they wanted and got on with it. When people enquired as to whether he was still in the priesthood he was hard at it and I know it was hard. People sometimes say to him, 'I'd love your faith', as if it was a matter of just having such faith by choice or getting such faith as a decision. Faith is earned, and built, and collected and grown and toiled for and lost and found again and prayed for and walked and talked and challenged and spat at and scary and difficult. Faith is increasingly in the margins like the person not asked to dance or rejected at the disco; faith can be lonely, faith is hard. For Bryan to have remained faithful to his Capuchin way of life for more than three decades when it would have been much easier to give up is testament to his strong faith. But it is not faith that fell from the sky or was easily or simply got, but faith that he has broken himself to hold on to.

Funnily enough, without even realising or comprehending the extent of the convenience, just as he has done for so many former students, friends and people in the parishes and communities he has served across the country, Bryan celebrated my wedding, baptised, confirmed and gave communion to my children. He came to the hospital and prayed with and blessed my daughter when she was ill. He has forever been at the beck and call of our family or anyone we request or nominate, but ironically, we've been the ones who have taken this unique privilege for granted and not articulated or acknowledged enough the pride we have in Bryan. When we were teenagers, we had a mutual best friend who was the only boy in his family. He was the one who nicknamed Bryan 'Bro'. One evening, as the three of us sat at a campfire in Kildare, he gave out to us for not understanding how lucky we were to have each other. Recently, too, a work colleague sent us a card thanking us because we arranged for Bryan to visit a sick relative of theirs. On the card was written: 'Bryan has changed our lives; you'll never know how much this means to our family'. The truth is we will never know, but we should count our blessings more.

His life was not and is not a waste, far from it, in fact the opposite. And I now know everyone knows it, which gives me comfort, but not because he forced them to acknowledge it or argued with them to believe it, but because his life speaks for itself. The Church needs more doers and fewer arguments, more actions and less talk. Even though it took over 30 years for me to realise something about him, it happened without me having to do anything. We need to get on with what we do and stop worrying about trying to correct others. Our actions alone will do what is needed and take us where we need to be.

God Bless Bryan

Kevin Shortall, 2019

Want to keep reading?

Columba Books has a whole range of books to inspire your
faith and spirituality.

As the leading independent publisher of religious and theological
books in Ireland, we publish across a broad range of areas including
pastoral resources, spirituality, theology, the arts and history.

All our books are available through
www.columbabooks.com
and you can find us on Twitter, Facebook and Instagram to discover
more of our fantastic range of books. You can sign up to our
newletter through the website for the latest news about events,
sales and to keep up to date with our new releases.

 columbabooks

 @ColumbaBooks

 columba_books